AF893783

# RETIREMENT WEALTH BY DESIGN

*Invest With Purpose, Leave Nothing to Chance, and Create a Retirement Plan That Gives You Financial Control for Life*

**BY TOM ELDER, CFP®**

Printed in the United States of America

First Printing, 2026

Cover and interior design by the Magellan Creative Team.

*This book is dedicated to:*

*My grandparents, father, and mother who showed me unconditional love and instilled faith, integrity, and work ethic through their actions and lessons.*

*My wife and children, all of whom continue to support me in our journey together as we navigate all of the twists and turns that happen, making our story together both unique and beautiful.*

*God who continues to teach and guide me down His path for me.*

# TABLE OF CONTENTS

# INTRODUCTION

*"Recognizing the need is the primary condition for design."*
*~ Charles Eames*

Working with my dad was like trying to crack a walnut using my bare hands. He just wouldn't open up. I would approach it from different sides, putting pressure on at different angles. I even tried using the financial tools that I had relied on over the years, calculators and investment reports and such. Still, it just wasn't working.

"When do you plan on retiring?" I asked.

"I don't," he replied.

"What happens if you can't work?" I followed up.

"I will work forever," he said. My dad wasn't joking. This was his truth.

So, things weren't going great so far. I felt shut down with every question I tried to ask.

Working with family members was always a different experience, so I had expected the challenge. Often it feels like they come into the meeting prepared to share their financial information, which I know was a tough decision for them to make. They bring in their statements and just kind of spread them all out and around the table, and then sit proudly back to read my reaction when I see what they have saved.

"This is great," I say. "You've done a good job." But then, when I ask the important questions, the questions that dive into purpose, goals, fears, and dreams, they clam up and become much more guarded than non-family members typically are.

This is what was happening now. My father sat across from

me, arms locked in front of his chest. The conversation had come to an impasse.

*Purpose, Tom, remember your purpose,* I told myself. Silently, I recited my purpose: *I am here to influence the community around me, and to leave folks better off financially because they met with me.*

Looking at my father, I suddenly wondered, what was his purpose? What did my dad really want out of retirement?

With nothing left to lose, I asked, “Why do you have your savings and retirement accounts if your plan is to work forever?” I wasn’t being cheeky—I really wanted to know. “What is the purpose of this money you have worked so hard to save? What do you want it to do for you?”

That was the right question to ask. My dad had thoughts about that. He leaned forward, uncrossed his arms, and started to talk. Now, we were getting to the heart of the matter.

Talking about money can make people nervous. Nearly two-thirds of American workers agree that preparing for retirement makes them feel stressed.[1] In my line of work, I find that once we define the purpose of the money, what we want it to do for us and where we want it to help us go, then we can work our way backwards. We can figure out if we are making the best investment decisions today to get us to our future destinations tomorrow. Reverse engineering, in a way.

That conversation with my father was enlightening to me. It was the first time I really articulated what made our firm so different. My father had worked with multiple financial advisors in the past, the most recent being someone who Dad had been with for over 10 years. My father shared with me how this advisor even wrote articles for the huge Wall Street firm that he worked for. However, my dad and I came to the conclusion that all the financial advisors he had worked with before were more of the *money manager* type broker dealers, because those advisors hadn’t discussed risk planning. They didn’t address the concerns

---

1 Employee Benefits Research Institute and Greenwald Research. 2025 Retirement Confidence Survey Fact Sheet: Preparing for Retirement in America. EBRI, April 2025. https://www.ebri.org/docs/default-source/rcs/2025-rcs/rcs_25-fs-3_prep.pdf?sfvrsn=f6e3042f_2, Accessed 11/21/2025.

specific to someone his age, and the concerns that everyone needs to think about once they near retirement. Issues such as:

- What if you were to get sick or couldn't work?
- How much income will you receive once you're retired?
- Do you have a tax strategy for your IRAs?
- Can you afford the cost of long-term care?
- Have you done legacy planning for your spouse, business, and kids?

My father's answer to all these questions was, "No," and yet, his money manager hadn't talked about any of them. All of these issues had been on his mind at one time or another and putting it all together seemed daunting to him. There were also many more items on the checklist that he hadn't thought about yet, and each one tied to a major concern of his.

For example, market loss. What if he experienced a major market crash just as he went to retire? He had been invested during the dot-com bubble in 2000-2002 and the mortgage crisis of 2008. Those losses were still fresh in his memory—when the market dropped more than 50 percent. Social Security was also something that he knew was important but had no idea where to find good advice about it.

It was all confusing, but this is what advisors like me do – we specialize in the concerns specific to people who are at or near retirement. I was able to show my dad that, thankfully, with his birthdate being what it was, he just barely qualified for a rule that would give him thousands of extra dollars in Social Security income. We were on our way toward getting him an income plan for retirement.

My dad was a great dad. As the father of four, he sacrificed for me and my brothers and sister for many years. My mom loved all four of us kids, was always there when we needed her, and is now there for my kids—her grandkids, who she loves, too. As a financial advisor, I wanted to be able to take care of my parents the way that they always took care of me—by removing obstacles, burdens, and stress so that they could focus on being who God made them to be.

The reason that I am a financial planner, though, comes from the generation before them. My grandfather taught me how to track stocks when I was 11 years old. He bought me my first financial calculator and showed me how to invest for the future. Although he passed away when I was a sophomore in college, I went on to earn my master's degree and to launch my own LLC.

My grandparents taught me that success in life isn't about the dollars in the bank or the title at the office; success is your ability to impact those around you. Furthermore, my grandparents taught me this lesson through their own actions, stories, and love. So, when I came to the point in my life that I realized I could have a major impact on my parents' lives, of whom I owed so much, I knew that I had found my purpose.

When I became a financial planner, I found phenomenal mentors, took hundreds of hours of coursework, worked on cases with experienced advisors, joined groups and organizations devoted to financial planning, and started meeting with thousands of people to discuss their financial situations. All of this was the forge that sharpened my skills and grew my knowledge so that I could connect with individuals to ask the right questions and give them applicable advice. In this way, I can help them to make educated financial decisions, with an understanding of the pros and cons. My path led me to become a CERTIFIED FINANCIAL PLANNER® and open an independent fiduciary business focused on retirement planning. Now, I focus on five key areas of financially planning for and in retirement – INCOME, INVESTMENTS, TAXES, HEALTHCARE, and LEGACY. Those are the five areas that we will cover in this book.

## Why Traditional Retirement Planning Isn't Enough for The Modern Retiree

Retirement is a concept that has evolved significantly over the decades. For many individuals, the idea of retirement has shifted from a simple cessation of work to a more complex lifestyle goal: financial independence, freedom, security, and ultimately, peace of mind so that you can focus on the important things in life and not have to watch and react daily to the stock market.

However, while retirement planning advice can easily be looked up on the internet, the advice is often conflicting. Gurus seem to give specific advice and yet make it sound applicable to everyone. The employer retirement plans of your parents' generation included pensions, healthcare plans, and Social Security. However, with the advent of 401(k)s, pensions have disappeared over time and the risk of investing for income has shifted from the company pension to the individual employee. According to an analysis of trends in savings, 61 percent of elderly households in the U.S. will face an income shortfall in retirement.[2] Running out of money is the top fear in retirement.[3] The available data suggests that defined contribution plans like the 401(k) are failing to help Americans achieve a secure retirement.[4]

As your 401(k) grew, the traditional retirement planning strategies fell short because major complexities were added. The considerations now are far more intricate, involving not just the basics of saving and withdrawing money, but the management of a multi-layered portfolio, tax strategies, legacy planning, and lifestyle choices. A modern retirement plan involves fundamental strategies that have proven to be successful for decades. It includes the addition of layers for future risks and concerns, and it shifts to ensure the money that you have saved is most efficiently used for the purpose that you have.

This introduction will explore why traditional retirement planning doesn't meet your needs anymore and why a more customized approach is necessary for those seeking to maximize their wealth and impact during this new phase of life.

---

2 ESI Econsult Solutions, INC, submitted to Pew Charitable Trusts, The Cost of Doing Nothing, May 2023, https://econsultsolutions.com/pew-federal-and-state-impacts-of-insufficient-retirement-savings Accessed 1/23/2024.

3 O'Brien, Elizabeth, Running Out of Money Is the Top Retirement Worry: Report, Barrons, June 2023, https://www.barrons.com/articles/money-top-retirement-worry-2830cc9f Accessed 8/15/2023.

4 "Plans, National Institute on Retirement Security, December 2023, https://www.nirsonline.org/2023/12/new-report-examines-impacts-of-switching-away-from-defined-benefit-pension-plans Accessed 8/04/2025.

## A One-Size-Fits-All Approach

Traditional retirement planning often follows a simple, one-dimensional framework: save, accumulate, and withdraw. The general advice is often based on a target income replacement rate, such as, "You will need to replace 70 to 80 percent of your pre-retirement income to maintain your standard of living." On the surface, that sounds simple enough, but there are many layers to it.

For instance, what happens if you want more from your savings than just income? What if you want to travel somewhere interesting? Which investments should you take from? Will you receive a big tax bill? What are the consequences of a large withdrawal to your Medicare premiums?

Americans are expected to spend around 29 years in retirement.[5] How long will the money last if you maintain your standard of living? How much do you need saved? What happens if you get sick? What happens if taxes increase while you are retired – do you just draw out more money?

Those online calculators that are on the internet or included on your 401(k) website can be helpful, but there are many variables that are often unaccounted for with them.

Sometimes I hear gurus say, "Nowadays, a person needs X amount of dollars—" and they throw out a number like $1 million, $2.6 million, or even $5 million—just to retire comfortably. Okay, but why? That sounds super generic and certainly cannot be true for everyone, but it gets clicks for the advertisers and publishers, so the information serves as a substitute for financial advice.

If we take it even a step further to consider the complexities of a larger amount saved, the desire for multi-generational wealth preservation, or the importance of leaving a legacy, minimizing tax liabilities becomes increasingly important. In fact, income taxes can be your single largest expense in retirement.[6] Since the passage of the SECURE Act, if you inherit a retirement account

5 Transamerica Center for Retirement Studies, Retiree Life in the Post-Pandemic Economy, Nov 2024, page 17, Retiree Life in the Post-Pandemic Economy | 24th Annual Transamerica Retirement Survey Accessed 1/09/2025.

6 FINRA, Taxation of Retirement Income, 2025, https://www.finra.org/investors/learn-to-invest/types-investments/retirement/managing-retirement-income/taxation-retirement-income Accessed 1/10/2025.

and you're not the spouse of the deceased, you must withdraw the entire account balance within 10 years of inheriting it. An estimated $15.75 billion in federal revenues will be generated from 2020 through 2029 due to the changes passed by this Act.[7] Ask yourself, who was this money supposed to be for? And what was your purpose when saving it?

Retirement planning only *begins* with having enough money to stop working. When you do it right, it's about making the most of existing wealth to ensure long-term sustainability, tax efficiency, and an enriching lifestyle in retirement.

## A Purposeful Approach to Retirement

Given the unique financial circumstances and aspirations of today's retiree, your approach to retirement must be tailored. It's no longer just about saving a certain percentage of income and withdrawing from retirement accounts when the time comes. Instead, successful retirement planning involves the following:

1. **Custom Investment Strategies:** Focusing on income-producing investments that align with individual risk tolerance and lifestyle needs. When income needs are fully met, money can then be set aside for significant growth and future goals.
2. **Tax-Advantage Planning:** Income-driven financial planning may also help reduce taxes. Implementing strategies to mitigate taxes throughout retirement, from tax-deferred growth to tax-efficient withdrawals and asset transfers, can help your money last longer.
3. **Legacy and Estate Planning:** A focus on not just securing one's own retirement but also ensuring wealth is passed to heirs in a tax-efficient manner will help stay true to the purpose of why you saved this money. This could involve the use of Roth IRAs, life insurance, family trusts, charitable giving, and other structures designed to maintain wealth for future generations.

7 Kurt, Daniel, What Is the SECURE Act and How Could It Affect Your Retirement? Investopedia, April 2024, https://www.investopedia.com/what-is-secure-act-how-affect-retirement-4692743 Accessed 9/20/2025.

4. **Flexibility and Control:** Designing a retirement plan that remains adaptable to personal goals and changing market conditions gives you freedom to spend. For example, a flexible drawdown strategy allows one to reduce withdrawals in times of market swings, or to strategically use debt to supplement income without selling off assets.

## Finding Your Sweet Spot

Retirement planning ultimately becomes a balancing act—one where a range of financial opportunities intersects with complex challenges. The decisions you make with this money today can significantly impact the trajectory of your retirement lifestyle, legacy, and wealth preservation.

This section will explore the specific financial challenges and opportunities faced by the modern retiree. From tax efficiency and investment strategy to risk management and estate planning, understanding these nuances is key to successfully navigating retirement with this level of wealth.

### *Unique Challenges*

When you are working in your 20s, 30s, and 40s, the goal of your savings is typically growth. You want your money to work as hard as you do to earn it. When growth is the goal, the traditional and well-known investment strategies can yield positive results. Sometimes more risk can yield more rewards when you are looking at the long term.

However, as you approach retirement, the *purpose* of this money often shifts from just pure growth to income needs or estate purposes. With this shift in purpose, the investments should also shift because the new goals present new challenges. However, most people working within the confines of the typical broker-dealer relationship are not getting access to the different types of financial tools that this shift requires.

*Tax Troubles*

Additionally, smart tax planning is essential for protecting your wealth in retirement. Without a solid plan, taxes on income, investments, and estate transfers can significantly reduce your savings. Retirement income comes from various sources like Social Security, pensions, investments, and rental properties. The One Big Beautiful Bill Act (OBBBA) did not change the rules for the taxation of Social Security. About 40 percent of people who receive Social Security will pay income taxes on their benefits.[8] Is your current advisor talking to you about these tax burdens and helping you to plan?

Without careful management, you could end up in a higher tax bracket, limiting your spending power. Capital gains taxes from selling stocks or real estate can also be costly, but strategies like tax-loss harvesting, charitable donations, and timing sales can wisely help lower your tax burden. Additionally, converting traditional retirement accounts to Roth IRAs can be a smart move for future tax savings, though it must be done strategically to avoid a major tax hit in the year of conversion. State taxes also play a big role, as high state income, property, and estate taxes can take a toll on your retirement funds, making location an important factor in planning.

***Not Running Out***

Beyond taxes, managing retirement income wisely ensures that savings last a lifetime. As you will see in Chapter Two, the traditional "4 Percent Rule" for withdrawing money may not work for everyone, as it doesn't account for market conditions, personal needs, or longevity. Healthcare costs, including long-term care, can be one of the biggest financial burdens in retirement, so planning ahead for these expenses is crucial.

Even with a strong savings plan, the risk of outliving assets is a real concern, especially for those who expect to live into their 80s and 90s. The biggest fear for older adults is the serious

---

8 SSA "Social Security Administration: Retirement Benefits" 2024 https://www.ssa.gov/pubs/EN-05-10035.pdf Page 11 Accessed 1/19/2024.

illness of a loved one.[9] Historically speaking, healthcare is the highest-inflated product on the market.[10] Rising costs, inflation, and market fluctuations must be factored in to ensure financial security for decades.

### *How to Get Growth*

Striking a balance between protecting and growing wealth is another key challenge. A well-diversified portfolio that includes a mix of stocks, bonds, annuities, real estate, and other investments can reduce risk while allowing for continued growth. Since market downturns are inevitable—likely occurring several times over a 20-year retirement—having a strategy to handle volatility is essential.

Safe withdrawal plans, maintaining cash reserves, and adjusting investments over time can help retirees stay financially secure, even during economic downturns. By proactively planning for taxes, income needs, and investment risks, retirees can enjoy financial stability and peace of mind throughout their golden years.

## Opportunities for Those Who Plan

While there are challenges, there are also unique opportunities for those who plan ahead. These opportunities arise from the flexibility that comes with wealth built through savings.

1. **Tax-Advantaged Investment Opportunities**
   You can take advantage of tax-advantaged accounts such as 401(k)s, IRAs, Roth IRAs, and Health Savings Accounts (HSAs). These vehicles allow for tax-deferred growth or tax-free withdrawals in retirement. Additionally, tax-efficient strategies such as charitable giving (donor-advised funds, qualified charitable distributions, charitable remainder trusts) can reduce taxable income and create a lasting legacy. With the recent passing of OBBBA, the standard

9 Senior Living, Top 10 Fears of Older Adults in 2024, https://www.seniorliving.org/finance/senior-fears-study Accessed 1/23/2024.

10 Rakshit, Shameek, et al, How does medical inflation compare to inflation in the rest of the economy? Peterson-KFF, Aug 2024, https://www.healthsystemtracker.org/brief/how-does-medical-inflation-compare-to-inflation-in-the-rest-of-the-economy/ Accessed 8/26/2025.

income tax deduction is larger, and Seniors get an extra $6,000 deduction per person through 2028.[11] The result? Retirees can often convert more money into a tax-free Roth without spilling into the next tax bracket.

2. **Philanthropy and Giving Back**
   For many individuals, philanthropy becomes an increasingly important part of retirement planning. With the financial resources to support causes close to their heart, these individuals can explore ways to integrate charitable giving into their estate plans. This may include setting up a private foundation, contributing to donor-advised funds, utilizing qualified charitable distributions, or using charitable trusts to reduce taxes while making a positive impact.
3. **Strategic Estate and Legacy Planning**
   Estate planning becomes increasingly important as wealth grows. Individuals often begin thinking about how to pass on wealth to their heirs while minimizing estate taxes and ensuring that their legacy is maintained as they get later in life, but planning for it early on can greatly enhance efficiency. Using trusts, tax-efficient gifting strategies, and life insurance policies to pass on wealth can help secure future generations' financial well-being.

The modern retirement presents a unique set of challenges and opportunities. While you may have a comfortable financial cushion, finding the sweet spot requires more sophisticated planning to navigate the complexities of tax efficiency, retirement income, and wealth preservation. You want to be able to enjoy retirement. That means balancing your desire for financial security with the flexibility to enjoy life and fulfill personal goals, all while managing the impact of taxes and long-term risks.

By recognizing these challenges and opportunities, you can create a retirement plan that not only ensures a steady income but also preserves your legacy, maximizes tax

11 IRS, One Big Beautiful Bill Act: Tax deductions for working Americans and seniors, July 2025, https://www.irs.gov/newsroom/one-big-beautiful-bill-act-tax-deductions-for-working-americans-and-seniors Accessed 9/02/2025.

advantages, and sets the stage for a fulfilling and financially secure retirement.

## The Goal of this Book

Retirement is a monumental phase in anyone's life. It is not simply about stepping away from work or ceasing to generate income. Retirement, in this context, is a unique opportunity to *design* a life that is as fulfilling as it is financially secure. This is an opportunity to balance personal desires, family legacy, and wealth preservation in a way that infinitely continues forward.

In this book, our goal is to empower you with the knowledge and tools to build a retirement plan that doesn't just safeguard your financial future but also aligns with your broader goals: a life of freedom, purpose, and a lasting legacy.

Whether you envision spending your golden years traveling the world, contributing to the causes you care about, spending time with you children/grandchildren or working in the garden, this book will provide you with strategic insights to make those dreams a reality. It will help you to design your retirement wealth plan on purpose, with purpose.

### *Define your Purpose by Designing your Lifestyle*

Retirement is an opportunity to create a lifestyle that is not constrained by the demands of work or the pressures of maintaining a certain income. This is where wealth becomes a powerful tool for designing a life filled with purpose, adventure, and fulfillment.

The first step in lifestyle design is a deep exploration of what you truly want out of retirement. This isn't just about what you'll do with your time, but also how you'll feel about your choices. Will you travel the world or invest in a second home? Do you plan to give back through charitable endeavors, or will you shift your focus to personal growth, hobbies, or spending more time with family?

The process of defining your retirement lifestyle requires understanding your desires in relation to your resources. We'll show you how to take your current wealth, income, and asset mix, and transform that into a tangible plan for enjoying your retirement years.

It's easy to think that retirement is only about how much you can spend, but true fulfillment comes from a balance between financial freedom and personal growth. You may have enough to live a comfortable lifestyle, but do you have a plan that ensures you're using your time in ways that bring joy and meaning? We'll explore strategies for ensuring that you strike the right balance between enjoying the present and preparing for an evolving future.

For many modern retirees, one of the most important aspects of retirement planning is crafting a legacy that extends far beyond their own lifetime. How you pass on your wealth—not just in terms of financial assets, but also values, experiences, and knowledge—can have a profound effect on your family and community. My grandfather did this for me, and I hope that you do this for your community and family around you.

You are at a pivotal moment in your life. Retirement is no longer a distant dream but an imminent reality—and now is the time to create a roadmap for the next chapter. By the end of this book, you'll be empowered with understanding and confidence to make decisions that will help you craft a retirement that isn't just financially secure but also personally and emotionally fulfilling.

The strategies outlined here aren't just about managing wealth; they're about designing a life and a legacy that lasts. Together, we'll explore how to create a retirement that enriches your life today and leaves a meaningful impact on the world long after you've stepped away from the workforce. It's time to start building the retirement you've always envisioned.

~ ***Tom Elder***, CERTIFIED FINANCIAL PLANNER® and President of Retirement Wealth Design, a holistic retirement planning firm serving residents of St. Lous, MO, and beyond.

## END OF CHAPTER CHALLENGE:

At the end of each chapter of this book will be a challenge. I encourage you to spend time thinking and writing the answers to the questions—and you can do so right in this book. The purpose is to reinforce what was discussed in the chapter, apply it to your specific situation, and advance your retirement plans forward.

Your first challenge begins now. Take a minute to contemplate the following questions.

Number the following in order of importance for yourself with number 1 being most important and 5 being least important.

__ Income Planning __ Tax Efficiency
__ Legacy/Estate Plan __ Investment Growth
__ Healthcare Costs

Rank your top concerns that could derail your retirement plan with number 1 being the most pressing concern.

__ Running out of money __ Rising inflation
__ Major market losses __ Tax increases
__ Major health incident __ Unexpected expenses
__ Financially supporting a parent/child/grandchild

Define the purpose of your money. Why do you have the savings that you have? What would you like this money to do for you?

________________________________________
________________________________________
________________________________________
________________________________________
________________________________________

Is charitable giving important to you to continue throughout retirement? If the answer is yes, how much and to whom would you give?

☐ YES ________________

☐ NO ________________

________________________________________________________________

________________________________________________________________

________________________________________________________________

________________________________________________________________

How do you plan to spend your time in retirement?

________________________________________________________________

________________________________________________________________

________________________________________________________________

________________________________________________________________

________________________________________________________________

# CHAPTER ONE

## THE PSYCHOLOGY OF WEALTH IN RETIREMENT

*"Doing well with money has a little to do with how smart you are and a lot to do with how you behave."*
*~ Morgan Housel*

"I have excellent news," I said joyfully to a client who we will call Mr. Baily. "It looks like you are on track to retire in two years!"

I had been excited to share this news with him because during our last meeting, he had told me that the soonest he would consider retiring was in two years. He also said, rather glumly, that he might just keep going for at least 10 years depending on the numbers. Now, he could retire without fear.

"Yeah," he said, shifting heavily in his chair. "I've been thinking about it, and I don't think that I want to retire in two years. I think I might just keep going as long as I can."

I waited, but Mr. Baily said this to me with absolutely no emotion on his face at all.

"No problem," I said. "I can respect that. But let's just go through what I have prepared, and hopefully, it will give you peace of mind to see that you at least have the option to retire in two years. If something changes at work, you get a boss you don't like or you change your mind, you'll know that you can just walk away and be OK."

Mr. Baily nodded, but before I got started, I had to ask him. "Do you mind sharing with me why the change of heart?"

Mr. Baily responded, "I don't know what I would do. I think I'd just be bored and then I would probably die early. That's what happened to my uncle—he retired and all he did was watch TV. A couple of years later, he was gone. I don't want that to happen to me."[12]

While Mr. Baily is a fictional name, he is not alone in feeling this way. I have found that not being psychologically prepared for retirement can be a very common obstacle to taking the leap into retired life. The reasons vary from emotional, to social, to financial, or other reasons. Planning ahead so that you can have a *purpose* in retirement is critical.

Sometimes it is helpful to identify your purpose before you retire. You might even get started while you are still working. For example, if you will be remodeling the basement in retirement, why not start now? It's going to be tiresome, but then when that retirement date hits, you are going to be even more excited, because now, you'll be on a fast track to get that project done.

It's interesting to see what people in retirement are actually hoping to do. According to the 2024 Transamerica Center for Retirement Studies, the top five retirement dreams among people in the middle class include the following:[13]

- Spending time with family and friends: 58 percent
- Pursuing hobbies: 51 percent
- Traveling: 67 percent
- Taking care of their grandchildren: 25 percent
- Doing volunteer work: 23 percent

Retirement is often seen as a financial goal, an endpoint that one reaches after years of hard work and saving. But for the modern retiree, retirement is not just about having the necessary funds to stop working; it's about navigating the deep psychological shifts that come with significant lifestyle changes, personal fulfillment, and the impact of wealth on decision-making.

As you approach retirement, your relationship with money, security, and success will change. The ability to manage

---

12 Based on a true story that has been fictionalized using figures believed to be reliable. Your own results may vary.

13 Transamerica Institute and Transamerica Center for Retirement Studies. The Retirement Outlook of the American Middle Class: 24th Annual Transamerica Retirement Survey. August 2024. https://www.transamericainstitute.org/docs/research/household-income/retirement-outlook-of-american-middle-class-survey-report-2024.pdf, Accessed 11/21/2025.

expectations, balance financial independence with the pursuit of personal fulfillment, and understand how wealth influences your choices is essential to crafting a rewarding and meaningful retirement. This chapter will delve into the psychological aspects of retirement, exploring how to manage the emotional and practical challenges that come with leaving the workforce, maintaining a sense of purpose, and using wealth as a tool for living a fulfilling life.

---

***Fast Fact:*** *Having a sense of purpose, nurturing relationships, and finding joy in everyday experiences all contribute to happiness, which in turn provides health benefits such as reduced stress, lower risk of chronic disease, improved immunity, and increased longevity.*[14]

---

## Managing Expectations for Lifestyle Changes

One of the biggest psychological hurdles for approaching retirement is managing expectations for lifestyle changes. For many, the idea of retirement evokes visions of leisurely days spent traveling, engaging in hobbies, and enjoying time with loved ones. But the reality often feels different, and the transition can be more jarring than anticipated.

The change from being immersed in the daily grind to having seemingly endless free time can be disorienting, especially when you've defined much of your identity through your work. For individuals who have been successful in their careers, retirement can feel like a loss of purpose. This sense of "who am I now?" can trigger anxiety and even a sense of existential crisis. The financial independence that retirement affords is often a double-edged sword, where freedom can be as overwhelming as it is liberating.

14 UMass Memorial Health, "Can Happiness Improve Health?," Simply Well Blog, April 2024, https://www.ummhealth.org/simply-well/can-happiness-improve-health, Accessed 9/10/2025.

To manage these shifts, it's crucial to develop realistic expectations and proactively plan for the changes in daily life. A great deal of emotional satisfaction comes from feeling productive and engaged, and if these needs are not addressed, boredom or dissatisfaction may set in. Many retirees—especially those with substantial wealth—find that they thrive when they adopt new goals, such as learning a new skill, volunteering, or mentoring younger generations. The key is not just to think about the logistics of wealth but also to consider how you'll channel your time and energy once the structure of your previous career is no longer there.

Another aspect of managing expectations in retirement is understanding the psychological importance of maintaining a healthy sense of self. Wealth can both help and hinder this. On one hand, it grants you the ability to focus on passions that were once sidelined by work obligations. On the other hand, extreme wealth can sometimes cause an individual to question what truly matters. It can lead to a distorted sense of self-worth, particularly if your self-image is heavily tied to professional achievement or the accumulation of assets.

Successfully navigating this phase requires redefining your identity in a more holistic way—one that is not solely defined by financial success. For many, retirement is an opportunity to cultivate new aspects of self-worth, such as the joy found in relationships, personal growth, and giving back to society. Finding a new "purpose" in retirement—whether it be through family, philanthropy, or personal projects—can be a deeply fulfilling experience, provided you take the time to assess your personal goals beyond money. John Maxwell once said, "I have never met a depressed person that was living for someone else, it is impossible."

Financial independence allows you the freedom to design your ideal lifestyle, but it also creates the potential for personal imbalance. Once you no longer need to worry about earning a living or accumulating wealth, how do you use your time and resources in ways that bring personal satisfaction and long-term happiness?

Many people assume that having more time and money equals more happiness. However, having an abundance of both can sometimes lead to a sense of aimlessness. When you have access to virtually everything you could want, it's easy to fall into a trap of excess, where material purchases or extravagant experiences no longer feel fulfilling.

To balance financial freedom with personal fulfillment, it's important to embrace the idea of intention. Just as your wealth allows you to afford certain luxuries, it also provides an opportunity to live with intention and meaning. Whether that means devoting time to travel with a sense of purpose, getting involved in causes that align with your values, or investing in creative projects that excite you, the goal should be to focus on experiences and pursuits that contribute to your personal growth and sense of purpose.

---

***Fast Fact:*** *Regularly volunteering has positive effects on depression, life satisfaction, and overall wellbeing.*[15]

---

## The Impact of Wealth on Choices

Financial independence opens the door to a broad range of options, and these choices can feel both exhilarating and overwhelming. However, wealth also influences decision-making in subtle ways, often leading to choices that might not align with true desires or values.

Wealth can sometimes distort the lens through which we view fulfillment. For example, having more financial resources can make it harder to distinguish between what you truly want and what is perceived as desirable due to societal expectations or external pressures. It can be easy to lose sight of what genuinely

15 Artushin, Heather Rose, Volunteering and Mental Health, Psychology Today, July 2025, https://www.psychologytoday.com/us/blog/well-read/202507/volunteering-and-mental-health Accessed 8/04/2025.

brings joy or meaning to your life when you are surrounded by abundance, both personally and socially.

Another critical aspect of wealth and retirement is the societal pressure to maintain a certain status or image. Many retirees worry that stepping away from their careers or scaling back their luxurious lifestyle might cause them to lose their social standing or relevance. However, true fulfillment in retirement comes from shedding these external pressures and redefining what success means to you personally, rather than allowing wealth or societal expectations to dictate your choices.

The best approach is to create a framework that balances financial freedom with introspection and personal values. Understanding how your wealth influences your choices and maintaining control over your decisions—rather than letting them be guided by external factors—ensures that your retirement choices align with what truly brings you happiness and contentment. When you find your proper balance, it leads to results.

About 67 percent of retirees who are 15 years or less into retirement said they're happier since retiring, and 82 percent said they're more relaxed on a typical day.[16] For many retirees, wealth in retirement is a tool to create meaningful and lasting experiences. Travel, art, culture, and philanthropy become not just ways to occupy time, but ways to enrich their lives and leave a legacy. These experiences can provide fulfillment and purpose that many traditional retirees may not be able to access. Whether it's donating to causes, starting a foundation, or traveling with loved ones to immersive destinations, wealth offers opportunities for enrichment that extends beyond financial security.

As wealth allows for more choices, it also creates challenges when deciding where to allocate your time and energy. For example, how much time should you dedicate to maintaining your properties, managing investments, or engaging in philanthropic/church endeavors? Balancing these decisions requires an

16 Cagnassola, Mary Ellen. "Not Everyone Is Happier After They Retire. Here's Why." Money, March 2024. https://money.com/retirement-happiness-study/, Accessed 9/23/2025.

awareness of what truly aligns with your personal goals and values. Wealth management, even in retirement, should not solely focus on preserving assets, but also on creating experiences that align with your vision of fulfillment and legacy.

---

***Fast Fact:*** *Americans who work with a financial advisor can retire, on average, two years sooner than those who don't work with an advisor.*[17]

---

## Conclusion

The psychology of wealth in retirement is complex. Financial independence opens a world of possibilities, but without careful thought and intentionality, it can lead to a sense of disconnection or aimlessness. By managing expectations for lifestyle changes, balancing financial freedom with personal fulfillment, and understanding the deep impact wealth has on retirement choices, you can craft a retirement that is not just financially secure but also personally meaningful and enriching.

The next phase of your life is a chance to redefine success and happiness—not through the lens of your career or the accumulation of wealth, but through a more holistic, intentional approach to living. Embrace the freedom wealth affords but remember that true fulfillment lies in living a life that reflects your values, your passions, and your deepest desires for the future.

17 Northwestern Mutual, Planning & Progress Study, 2024, Value of an Advisor, https://news.northwesternmutual.com/planning-and-progress-study-2024 Accessed 1/23/2025.

## CHAPTER ONE CHALLENGE:

How will your lifestyle change in retirement with your friends, family, and spending habits?

How will you define your own "success" during retirement?

How will you make your days meaningful and use your time and energy?

How will you "invest" in yourself with experiences that align with your values?

How can you create structure in your lifestyle during retirement?

# CHAPTER TWO

## THE MODERN RETIREMENT DILEMMA

*"There's gotta be a better way to save for retirement than using something where half your money can disappear almost overnight and there's nothing you can do about it."*
*~ From the documentary-style movie,*
*The Baby Boomer Dilemma*

Kevin was 67 years old and married to Stephanie, age 65. Stephanie had retired about two months before they began meeting with me, and I remember them because they had come to see me for a second opinion. I'm a big advocate of the second opinion, but most folks don't bother putting in the effort. I was impressed that Kevin and Stephanie had taken the time to meet with me, even after working with their current advisor for the last eight years.

"So, tell me what brought you here?" I asked.

They explained that, while they hadn't heard from their advisor too often, recently Stephanie had been feeling pressure from him. He wanted her to move the rest of her 401(k) over to one of his proprietary investment accounts. When she asked him, "If I do that, will we have enough to retire?" He told her, "Yes! You will be okay."

"That is great news!" I said. "So, tell me about your plan." I asked this knowing that, while many Americans were saving for retirement, nearly half of them did not have a written plan.[18] So, I was hoping, since they were working with an advisor, that they might have one.

---

18 Alliance Center for the Future of Retirement, How Americans feel about retirement in 2025, Study, July 2025, page 4, https://www.allianzlife.com/-/media/Files/Global/documents/2025/07/22/09/10/EXT-1127.pdf Accessed 8/11/2025.

Kevin replied, "Well, I think that we are going to relax for a little while, and then we might take a celebratory, extended vacation down to Florida. I've always wanted to see a rocket launch in person."

"Yes, Florida is excellent this time of year," I endured, "especially if you have the freedom to travel." I shifted in my chair. "What I was inquiring about, however, was more of your financial plan. Where is the money coming from? How much will you have to spend? How long will it last? ... that sort of thing."

Kevin responded rather quickly

"Ahh, yes, well, that is why we are here. You brought up a lot of great questions in your workshop, questions that have been on my mind. When we asked our advisor about it, he said that he doesn't really do that sort of work, and that we should ..."

Stephanie cut him off mid-sentenced.

"I didn't get a great feeling from him. When we asked him which accounts the money was coming from, he just responded, 'Well, how much do you need?' And he told me he would send it to me."

They looked at each other, concerned. I interjected at this point.

"Well, I'm sure that he has a way to do this for you. Did you work through an income plan together? A projection of how much money you would be receiving when you retired? And how long that would last?"

Again, they looked at each other with even more concern.

The answer was no.

Later, I later found out that not only did they *not* have an income plan, but they had invested nearly *all* their money in stocks, despite the fact that they were not comfortable with the **risk**. Even worse, they hadn't even realized how exposed they were until we reviewed it.

In addition, they were concerned about taxes because all their savings had accumulated in **traditional IRAs**. Stephanie and Kevin also had a special needs child with no estate transfer plan in place, and yet, they were both already retired!

Rolling up my sleeves, we got to work. Our first area of focus was how to manage the 401(k) for Stephanie's retirement income.

- We replaced her take-home pay from when she was working.
- This income would stay the same in good markets and bad.
- She knew where the money would come from and how much the check would be.
- We also adjusted for **inflation** to give her pay raises as needed.
- We determined the optimum time for her to take her Social Security benefit.
- We balanced their investments so that they were both comfortable with how much they could lose if the market dropped, and what their expected rate of return would be over time

When we were done, they both looked at each other with amazement on their faces. Finally, they felt financially free. They knew what their income would be, it was secured forever, and it would begin immediately. Yet, we only used 60 percent of their retirement savings!

Next, we focused on the design of a tax strategy, repositioning some of their savings so that more of their money would be theirs to keep. At the same time, they set-up a meeting with a recommended attorney who specialized in **estate planning** for special needs trusts. This ensured their child would be well taken care of.

The other 40 percent of their savings was going to be used for both *fun* and *future planning* in retirement, such as that trip to Florida, and to fund the special needs trust so that their child would continue to receive state and federal support for care even when she inherited the money. Best of all, we set it up so their daughter would inherit this money tax-free.[19]

---

19 Based on a true story that has been fictionalized using figures believed to be reliable. Your own results may vary.

Retirement represents so much more than the end of a career or the ability to stop working. It is an opportunity to live life on your own terms, secure your family's future, and leave a lasting legacy. But with this privilege comes significant complexity. Retirement planning involves navigating risks that can threaten wealth preservation, disrupt retirement goals, and compromise long-term financial stability.

In this chapter, we will explore the key challenges facing those who are planning for retirement. Retirement planning is not the same for everyone. As your wealth grows higher over time, it comes with more significant risks—risks that must be carefully managed to ensure financial security.

Three primary risks that stand out are: taxes, inflation, and market volatility. These risks threaten not only the ability to generate sufficient income in retirement but also the ability to preserve wealth for future generations. We will unpack the complexities surrounding these risks, including wealth preservation across generations.

Additionally, we'll examine the crucial distinction between *financial security* and *financial freedom*, and why understanding this difference can be the key to ensuring a fulfilling retirement.

---

***Fast Fact:*** *Retirees who took steps to set themselves up financially at least five years prior to retirement are more likely to report being much happier in retirement.*[20]

---

## Taxes—the Silent Eroder

Quick question—what's the highest tax rate ever paid by Americans? The answer: 94 percent.[21] Imagine paying 94

20 MassMutual. 2024 MassMutual Retirement Happiness Study. Massachusetts Mutual Life Insurance Company, 2024. https://www.massmutual.com/global/media/shared/doc/2024_massmutual_retirement_happiness_study.pdf, Accessed 6/10/2025.

21 Tax Policy Center, Historical Highest Marginal Income Tax Rates, May 2023, https://www.taxpolicycenter.org/statistics/historical-highest-marginal-income-tax-rates Accessed 8/11/2025.

percent! This was the top federal income tax rate in 1944, and it remained in the 50 to 90 percent range until it went down in 1987 to 38.50 percent. In 2025, the highest marginal tax rate was 37 percent, but tax rates are changing all the time.

How high will they go during a 30-year retirement?

One of the most significant threats to wealth in retirement is taxes. While taxes are a universal concern, for those that have saved most of their career, they can be far more complex and costly. This is especially true if, like Stephanie, you've saved in a 401(k). This is a type of tax-deferred account, which means the money comes out of your paycheck *before* this income is taxed, grows *without* being taxed, and it continues to *grow without being taxed,* compounding interest. This allows you to accumulate a nice big pot of money.

Now, the closer you get to the time of retirement, the bigger that pot of money grows. For most people, their IRA or 401(k) is the single largest monetary account they own. You might also have a 403(b), 457, or a Thrift Savings Plan (TSP), but those are just other examples. The majority of people who save for retirement do so in tax-deferred accounts.

The problem? You haven't paid any taxes on this money. Not on the amount you initially put in, and not on the growth. Unless this money sits inside a **Roth IRA**, *you still owe income tax on every penny of what you have saved.*

That means Uncle Sam gets a certain percentage of every dollar you take out. In retirement, income taxes, estate taxes, capital gains taxes, and property taxes can erode wealth if not planned for carefully. These taxes can take a huge bite out of retirement savings, leaving less money available for lifestyle expenses, legacy goals, or long-term financial growth.

Let's examine the four types of taxes you'll encounter.

- **Income Taxes:** Many retirees rely on a combination of income sources during retirement, such as Social Security, stock dividends, rental income, pension distributions, or withdrawals from retirement accounts. Each of these income streams is taxable at different rates. In some cases, additional taxes may apply depending on your location and the type of income you're receiving. The cumulative effect can result in a tax burden that significantly reduces your available cash flow.

- **Capital Gains Taxes:** If your wealth is tied up in investments—whether stocks, bonds, or real estate—these are taxable assets. Selling assets can trigger capital gains taxes. With long-term holdings, you can benefit from a lower tax rate, but large capital gains can still substantially reduce your after-tax income, especially if you sell off appreciated assets in retirement.
- **Estate Taxes:** The ability to transfer wealth efficiently to heirs is a key concern for modern retirees. With high estate tax exemptions in place, many retirees will be able to pass down wealth without paying estate taxes. However, if the estate grows beyond the exemption limits, taxes could erode a significant portion of the inheritance. Estate planning strategies like **trusts**, charitable giving, and other wealth transfer tools become essential in mitigating these risks.
- **State and Local Taxes:** Depending on where you live in retirement, state and local taxes can dramatically increase your tax burden. Some states have high income, property, and estate taxes, while others—like Florida, Texas, and Nevada—are tax-friendly. There were only nine states that taxed your Social Security income in 2025, down from 13 just a few years ago. Your advisor should keep track of the tax law changes for your state. Relocation to a state with lower tax rates could provide significant financial benefits.

While you have zero control over tax law and what Congress does, you do have 100 percent control over what you do with this money. That is the difference between planning for vs. paying your taxes, and we will be talking more about this in Chapter Five.

## STRATEGY TIP

To mitigate the tax burden in retirement, tax diversification becomes a vital strategy. By holding a mix of tax-deferred, tax-free, and taxable assets, you can better manage your withdrawals and income generation, adjusting for tax implications based on your needs and the prevailing tax laws.

### Inflation: The Hidden Erosion of Purchasing Power

Between 2007 and 2009, Zimbabwe entered a deep economic crisis. Land reform policies seized and redistributed farms to people with little farming experience. This then led to a sharp decline in agricultural production, drastic escalation of the national debt, significant governmental corruption, paired with a decline in industrial output.

To respond to these problems, the government of Zimbabwe began printing more money instead of implementing economic reforms. Printing more money resulted in hyperinflation peaking in November 2008 at an annual rate of 89.7 sextillion percent, which, if you can imagine, is 89.7 followed by 20 zeros. Prices doubled every 24.7 hours! The Zimbabwean dollar became worthless because people needed trillions just to buy basic goods like bread and soap.

The central bank then started issuing a 100 trillion Zimbabwean dollar note. Finally, people abandoned the local currency and switched to U.S. dollars, the South African rand, and bartering. The hyperinflation only officially ended when Zimbabwe's government changed to a multi-currency system based on the U.S. dollar.

Inflation is often an afterthought when planning for retirement, but it is one of the most dangerous risks to long-term financial security. Over time, inflation can gradually erode the purchasing power of your savings, even if the nominal value of your portfolio remains unchanged. For retirees who expect to live for 20 years or more, the cumulative effects of inflation can significantly impact the value of their assets and their ability to maintain their standard of living.

- **Healthcare Costs:** Healthcare inflation is a particular concern. As medical expenses continue to rise at rates far exceeding general inflation, retirees must ensure they have sufficient funds to cover long-term care needs and medical bills. Medicare Part B premiums continue to rise faster than inflation and the Cost-of-Living-Adjustments (COLA) to Social Security. From 2005 to 2024, Part B premiums increased an average of 5.5 percent each year while COLA averaged 2.6 percent.[22]
- **Cost of Living:** Even if inflation does not rise dramatically in the near term, general increases in the cost of living—such as housing, food, and energy—can have a significant impact on retirement income. The targeted inflation rate is 2 percent, but the current long-term average is 3.28 percent, which means prices will double every 20 years.[23] Retirees may find that their initial retirement budgets need to be revised due to rising prices.
- **Investment Impact:** As inflation rises, it reduces the real value of your investment returns. A five percent return in an inflationary environment of three percent only provides a two percent *real* return. This is why building an investment strategy that can outpace inflation is essential for those with significant wealth.

22 Lee, Medora, 2025 Medicare Part B premium increase outpaces both Social Security COLA and inflation, USA Today, Nov 2024, https://www.usatoday.com/story/money/personalfinance/2024/11/11/2025-medicare-part-b-premiums-rise/76186664007/ Accessed 8/11/2025.

23 US Inflation Rate (I:USIR) updated Nov 2023, https://ycharts.com/indicators/us_inflation_rate#:~:text=Basic%20Info,in%20price%20over%20a%20year. Accessed 1/03/2024.

Even when inflation rates are low, the effect is felt more by retirees, many of whom live on a fixed income. Therefore, it's not just important that you grow your money every year during retirement; you also want to grow your income. Retirement income should not be stagnant. It needs to increase each year just like prices increase each year.

### STRATEGY TIP

To protect against inflation, consider inflation-linked investments such as Treasury Inflation-Protected Securities (TIPS), real estate, or commodities. Additionally, building a diversified portfolio that includes both growth and income-generating assets will help combat the purchasing power erosion caused by inflation.

## Market Volatility: Navigating the Ups and Downs

While the stock market historically provides long-term growth, it is subject to volatility. Volatility describes the degree to which the value of an asset can fluctuate in price. This can pose a serious threat to retirement plans, particularly for individuals who are dependent on their investment portfolio, selling these assets for income.

### *The Math of Loss in Retirement*

Most people think that if you experience a 50 percent loss, you will be made whole with a 50 percent return.

In retirement, if a portfolio has $1,000,000 in it, and the market drops by 50 percent, that portfolio will now have

$500,000. If the next year the market grows by 50 percent, the growth is only on the current $500,000 balance, so the account total is only $750,000.

In other words, the investor is in the hole by -$250,000 even though they have averaged a zero percent average return. Take a look at the simplified visual using quarters below:

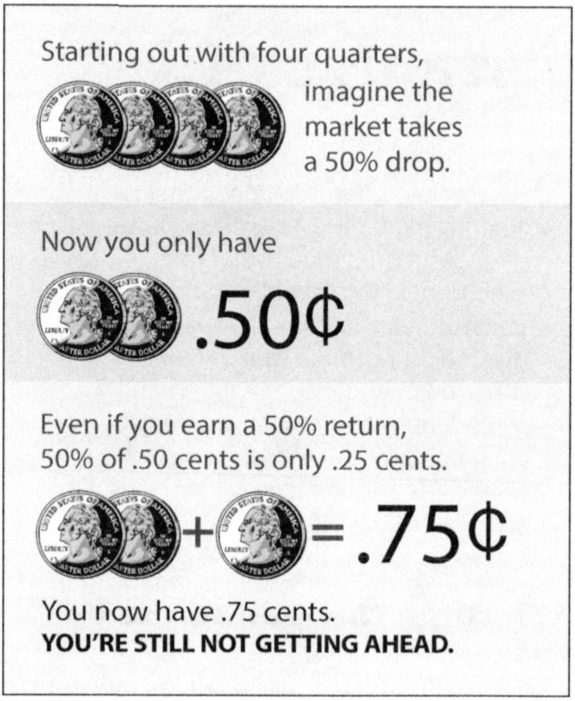


Source: Magellan Financial. Not indicative of investment performance.

***Sequence of Returns Risk***

A market downturn in the early years of retirement—when assets are being liquidated to fund living expenses—can lead to significant financial strain. This is when *the order* or *sequence* of investment returns becomes more important than the average rate of return. If a retiree experiences a market downturn early in retirement, it can significantly reduce the value of their portfolio, forcing them to withdraw more to cover living expenses and potentially jeopardizing long-term financial security.

This happens because once you are withdrawing money, you experience loss differently. The modern retiree doesn't have time to recover the losses when they withdraw income. If you are near retirement or have recently retired, a big hit to your portfolio can cripple it for the rest of your life. Whereas if you have 20 years to keep saving and investing, or if you are well into your retirement and have protected most of your assets from market risk, a market downturn wouldn't affect you as much.

Take, for example, the two sisters who retired with the same portfolio valued at $1 million, earning the same rate of return at 5.9 percent, and withdrawing the same income of $50,000 a year. Both sisters saw the *exact same down years*, only the *sequence* or order of the returns was reversed.

- Sister One saw her down years during her first few years in retirement.
- Sister Two experienced those *exact same down years*, but later.

The result?

At the end of the 25-year period between 2000 and 2024, Sister One had run out of money, whereas Sister Two had a balance of over $2 million. Take a look on the next page.

## SISTER ONE

Account balance after 24 years: -$193,544

**SP 500 YEAR 2000 -2024**

Assuming 50K annual withdrawal

| | Beg. Of Year Acct. Value | End Of Year Acct. Value | Earnings Rate |
|---|---|---|---|
| 2000 | $1,000,000.00 | $848,600.00 | -10.14% |
| 2001 | $848,600.00 | $687,942.56 | -13.04% |
| 2002 | $687,942.56 | $477,170.38 | -23.37% |
| 2003 | $477,170.38 | $553,047.93 | 26.38% |
| 2004 | $553,047.93 | $552,766.94 | 8.99% |
| 2005 | $552,766.94 | $519,349.95 | 3.00% |
| 2006 | $519,349.95 | $540,085.41 | 13.62% |
| 2007 | $540,085.41 | $509,150.43 | 3.53% |
| 2008 | $509,150.43 | $263,178.43 | -38.49% |
| 2009 | $263,178.43 | $274,893.77 | 23.45% |
| 2010 | $274,893.77 | $260,025.19 | 12.78% |
| 2011 | $260,025.19 | $210,025.19 | 0.00% |
| 2012 | $210,025.19 | $188,189.57 | 13.41% |
| 2013 | $188,189.57 | $193,893.68 | 29.60% |
| 2014 | $193,893.68 | $165,978.17 | 11.39% |
| 2015 | $165,978.17 | $114,766.53 | -0.73% |
| 2016 | $114,766.53 | $75,715.26 | 9.54% |
| 2017 | $75,715.26 | $40,419.16 | 19.42% |
| 2018 | $40,419.16 | -$12,102.99 | -6.24% |
| 2019 | -$12,102.99 | -$46,504.66 | 28.88% |
| 2020 | -$46,504.66 | -$88,077.60 | 16.26% |
| 2021 | -$88,077.60 | -$115,025.74 | 26.89% |
| 2022 | -$115,025.74 | -$187,386.74 | -19.44% |
| 2023 | -$187,386.74 | -$191,982.94 | 24.23% |
| 2024 | -$191,982.94 | -$193,544.70 | 23.31% |

**AVG RETURN 5.90%**

Source: Magellan Financial. For illustrative purposes only based on the S&P 500 Index from the years 2000 to 2024. The results presented above do not represent any actual investment performance or the actual account of our investors. Standard and Poor's 500 index is a capitalization weighted index of 500 stocks. The index is designed to measure performance of the broad domestic economy through changes in the aggregate market value of 500 stocks representing all major industries. Investors cannot invest directly in an index. Index returns do not reflect any fees, expenses, or sales charges.

## SISTER TWO

Account balance after 24 years: $2,268,377

### SP 500 YEAR 2024 -2000

Assuming 50K annual withdrawal

| Year | Beg. Of Year Acct. Value | End Of Year Acct. Value | Earnings Rate |
|---|---|---|---|
| 2024 | $1,000,000.00 | $1,183,100.00 | 23.31% |
| 2023 | $1,183,100.00 | $1,419,765.13 | 24.23% |
| 2022 | $1,419,765.13 | $1,093,762.79 | -19.44% |
| 2021 | $ 1,093,762.79 | $1,337,875.60 | 26.89% |
| 2020 | $1,337,875.60 | $1,505,414.18 | 16.26% |
| 2019 | $1,505,414.18 | $1,890,177.79 | 28.88% |
| 2018 | $1,890,177.79 | $1,722,230.70 | -6.24% |
| 2017 | $1,722,230.70 | $2,006,687.90 | 19.42% |
| 2016 | $2,006,687.90 | $2,148,125.92 | 9.54% |
| 2015 | $2,148,125.92 | $2,082,444.60 | -0.73% |
| 2014 | $2,082,444.60 | $2,269,635.04 | 11.39% |
| 2013 | $2,269,635.04 | $2,891,447.02 | 29.60% |
| 2012 | $2,891,447.02 | $3,229,190.06 | 13.41% |
| 2011 | $3,229,190.06 | $3,179,190.06 | 0.00% |
| 2010 | $3,179,190.06 | $3,535,490.55 | 12.78% |
| 2009 | $3,535,490.55 | $4,314,563.08 | 23.45% |
| 2008 | $4,314,563.08 | $2,603,887.75 | -38.49% |
| 2007 | $2,603,887.75 | $2,645,804.99 | 3.53% |
| 2006 | $2,645,804.99 | $2,956,163.63 | 13.62% |
| 2005 | $2,956,163.63 | $2,994,848.54 | 3.00% |
| 2004 | $2,994,848.54 | $3,214,085.42 | 8.99% |
| 2003 | $3,214,085.42 | $4,011,961.16 | 26.38% |
| 2002 | $4,011,961.16 | $3,024,365.84 | -23.37% |
| 2001 | $3,024,365.84 | $2,579,988.53 | -13.04% |
| 2000 | $2,579,988.53 | $2,268,377.69 | -10.14% |

**AVG RETURN 5.90%**

Source: Magellan Financial. For illustrative purposes only based on the S&P 500 Index from the years 2000 to 2024. The results presented above do not represent any actual investment performance or the actual account of our investors. Standard and Poor's 500 index is a capitalization weighted index of 500 stocks. The index is designed to measure performance of the broad domestic economy through changes in the aggregate market value of 500 stocks representing all major industries. Investors cannot invest directly in an index. Index returns do not reflect any fees, expenses, or sales charges.

While you have no control over the sequence of returns, you do control the allocation of your money. If you want to remain in the market during retirement, it might be necessary to change your investment strategy. Considerations might include whether you need this money to cover all or some of your income needs and how near or far you are away from retirement.

***Recession and Economic Cycles***

While the market generally trends upward over the long term, economic cycles—including recessions and bear markets—are inevitable. Market corrections with declines between 10 percent and 20 percent happen every two years on average.[24]

As we learned at the beginning of this section, once your account loses, the compounding muscle of your portfolio becomes crippled. You're no longer starting with the same base amount, and so it takes more investment energy to restore your account to its previous vigor. It also takes more time.

---

***Fast Fact:*** *It took over a decade for the average investor practicing a traditional buy-and-hold strategy to get back to even after experiencing the market loss of 2008.*[25]

---

Retirees may not be insulated from these cycles, and portfolio strategies must account for the potential of market downturns and prolonged periods of low returns.

24 Guggenheim Investments, Putting Pullbacks in Perspective–White Paper, Fall 2024, https://www.guggenheiminvestments.com/advisor-resources/crucial-conversations-client-facing Accessed 1/09/2025.

25 Arnott, Amy, How Long Will it Take the Market to Recover? Morningstar, Jan 2023, https://www.morningstar.com/portfolios/how-long-will-it-take-market-recover Accessed 1/10/2024.

## STRATEGY TIP

To protect against market volatility, it's important to have a strategy that includes diversification, a solid emergency cash reserve, and a flexible withdrawal plan that adjusts according to market conditions. Using fixed-income investments or annuities can provide stability during turbulent times.

### Preserving Wealth Across Generations: The Legacy Dilemma

Beyond the immediate concerns of retirement income and lifestyle maintenance, many modern retirees are equally focused on preserving their wealth across generations. While you may have accumulated a significant amount of wealth, without the right planning, it can be easily eroded through taxes, poor investment decisions, or lack of effective wealth transfer strategies.

- **Family Education and Involvement:** One of the most critical elements of successful wealth transfer is ensuring that future generations are educated on managing and preserving wealth. Dubbed the "Great Wealth Transfer," studies estimate that $84.4 trillion in assets will be passed down in the next two decades.[26] Many families fall into the trap of passing down wealth without preparing heirs for the responsibilities that come with it. Incorporating financial education into family discussions and involving heirs in planning can help ensure that the wealth is managed prudently.

26 Milken Institute, We Aren't Talking Enough About One Aspect of the Great Wealth Transfer, July 2024, https://milkeninstitute.org/content-hub/power-ideas-essays/we-arent-talking-enough-about-one-aspect-great-wealth-transfer Accessed 9/04/2024.

- **Philanthropy:** Charitable giving is another powerful tool for both wealth transfer and reducing tax burdens. By setting up charitable trusts, donor-advised funds, or foundations, individuals can ensure that their wealth has a positive impact on the causes they care about, while simultaneously reducing the taxable portion of their estate.

A legacy is about more than just getting the right stuff to the right people; it's about ensuring that your wishes are carried out in the manner you choose. This goes beyond just financial objects to include your relationships and the care for the people who you love. A solid estate plan will include components that allow you to accomplish both.

**STRATEGY TIP**

To preserve wealth across generations, it's essential to have a well-structured estate plan that includes trusts, tax-efficient gifting strategies, and a legacy that aligns with family values. Working with an estate planner or attorney can help ensure that wealth is passed down effectively, and in a tax-efficient manner.

## Financial Security vs. Financial Freedom: Understanding the Difference

A key distinction for the modern retiree is understanding the difference between financial security and financial freedom.

- **Financial Security:** This is about having enough wealth to meet your basic needs and ensure a stable, comfortable retirement. It's about not running out of money, which is the number one concern of retirees regardless of their portfolio size. Even for those that have financial security, money alone may not be enough to provide the lifestyle freedom or legacy goals that many desire.

- **Financial Freedom:** Financial freedom goes beyond security. It is the ability to live life on your own terms, free from financial constraints. This means having the freedom to pursue your passions, give back, and enjoy the experiences that make life meaningful. It's about having the flexibility to make choices based on what matters to you, rather than being driven solely by financial necessity.

As an advisor, what I want for you and all my clients is financial freedom. Achieving this freedom requires careful planning to ensure not only that you have enough assets to meet your needs but also that your wealth is structured to provide flexibility for pursuing personal goals, philanthropic endeavors, and family aspirations.

It also is heavily weighted on mindset. When a retiree understands their plan and the path that they are financially on, often times that can free their mind from the restraints of feeling like they're "running out of money" so they can now focus on the important things in life and live financially free.

---

***Fast Fact:*** *Nearly 90% of annuity owners worry less about retirement, and 75% say they have more money for discretionary spending.*[27]

---

## Conclusion

As you plan for retirement, understanding the risks and complexities at play is critical. Taxes, inflation, market volatility, and the need for effective wealth transfer are all issues that high-net-worth individuals must address if they hope to create a retirement that is both financially secure and personally

27 New York Life Research, June 2023, https://www.newyorklife.com/newsroom/annuity-owners-report-spending-more-staying-invested-and-feeling-happier-in-retirement Accessed 1/10/2025.

fulfilling. By carefully navigating these risks and understanding the distinction between financial security and freedom, you can design a retirement that meets your lifestyle goals, preserves your legacy, and enables you to enjoy the freedom you've worked so hard to achieve.

## CHAPTER TWO CHALLENGE:

Rank your financial confidence on a scale of 1 to 10 (with 10 being the most confident, and 1 being the least confident) by circling one of the numbers below. If you ranked yourself less than a 10, consider getting a second opinion.

0 1 2 3 4 5 6 7 8 9 10

Does your retirement plan include a Strategic Tax Plan? What is the plan?

____________________________________________

____________________________________________

____________________________________________

____________________________________________

Does your retirement plan include income accounting for inflation? How much inflation?

____________________________________________

____________________________________________

____________________________________________

____________________________________________

Does your plan include what to do when the market crashes? How are you set up proactively so that you aren't responding reactively when it occurs?

____________________________________________

____________________________________________

____________________________________________

Does your plan include an efficient estate transfer? What is currently in place and what needs to be done?

________________________________________________________
________________________________________________________
________________________________________________________
________________________________________________________

If you plan to give charitably during retirement or post-mortem, what tax-saving strategies are you going to leverage?

________________________________________________________
________________________________________________________
________________________________________________________
________________________________________________________

Getting interviewed by a qualified financial planner can bring clarity to what is important to you, crystalize your concerns, and establish goals for your future. If you have not been interviewed and would like a complimentary session to gain more clarity around your retirement plan, please use any of the three contact options below to schedule with us.

- By phone: (636) 388-7722
- By email: Info@RetirementWealthDesign.com
- Visit our website at: RetirementWealthDesign.com

# CHAPTER THREE

## THE FIVE BIG INCOME CHALLENGES

*"Don't simply retire from something; have something to retire to."*
*~ Harry Emerson Fosdick*

In the past, people often looked forward to retiring at age 65. They might have received a pension, a gold watch, and enjoyed a relaxing retirement for about 10 years. But today, retirement is different. People are living longer, staying healthier, and staying active. Many continue working after age 65, starting new careers, or switching in and out of jobs.

At the same time, traditional retirement income, like Social Security or pension plans, are changing. This means retirees face new challenges in making sure they have enough money for their future. The responsibility for having a comfortable retirement now falls mostly on the individual.

Because of these changes, planning for retirement has become more important than ever. One of the biggest challenges is figuring out how to make sure retirement income lasts a lifetime. You must plan for a long retirement, understand the rules for taking money out of retirement accounts, and do your best to insulate that money from the many risks that you will face through retirement. Whether you are younger than 59½, older than 73, or somewhere in between, it's important to take care of your retirement money properly. After all, it is your life savings.

This chapter will explore how retirement has changed and why more people are focused on the money they'll need during retirement. It will also look at strategies to help people get the most out of their retirement income.

***Fast Fact:*** *Having a higher actual income was linked with higher sense of purpose, greater personal growth, greater self-acceptance, greater environmental mastery as well as higher life satisfaction and fewer negative emotions.*[28]

## Income Planning Challenges for the Modern Retiree

Here are some of the things people have told me over the years as they think about preparing for retirement:

*"I have kind of been on autopilot the last 30 years, but now that I turned 60, I realize I need to start making some changes to get ready for retirement."*

*"I have so many questions. It seems like the more that I read online, the further down these rabbit holes I go, and they all contradict each other."*

*"I am pretty confident; I used a calculator online and it said that I was in good shape. I just wanted to get together for a second opinion."*

*"I just need help!"*

I have heard all these responses and thousands more when first meeting with people. Whatever your concern, there is no "typical" starting point; you start where you are now.

The caveat is that in order to know how to get where you are going, first we need to figure out where you are now, and then we need to determine where your destination will be. It's just like using GPS on your phone. We need the starting point of the trip and the destination of the trip, then we can determine the best route to get there. This is because everyone's retirement journey looks different.

In my experience, there is no "in today's world you need X

28 University of Wisconsin–Madison. "Is What You Believe About Whether Money Buys Happiness as Important as Having Money?" October 2024. https://aging.wisc.edu/2024/10/22/is-what-you-believe-about-whether-money-buys-happiness-as-important-as-having-money. Accessed 10/2/2025.

dollars to retire comfortably." Depending on the guru, they could advertise that you need $1 million, $2 million, $5 million—really, anything! But does the person that is living comfortably on Social Security alone really need $5 million dollars?! Probably not.

Just like the person with four homes, two mortgages, and living on a monthly expense budget of $50,000, they will still have fears about running out of money. For them, $5 million might not be enough. It's all relative to your individual lifestyle.

In many ways, financially planning for retirement demands a higher level of attention than ever before. Workers can no longer assume that a company pension will be waiting for them at 65. The burden of your future finances was placed on your shoulders instead of the company's when pensions began to get eliminated. And, as of writing this book, there grows an uncertainty around the future of Social Security benefits amongst retirees.

This all requires making investment decisions that become increasingly complicated and diverse. We must plan proactively for retirement to minimize taxes, continue to grow our **principal**, ensure our money lasts forever, and leave as much behind for the next generation while also fulfilling our ambitions. This all begins, as a cornerstone, with how we are going to take the money out and pay ourselves through retirement.

---

***Fast Fact:*** *80% of retirees worry about changes that could reduce their Social Security benefit.*[29]

---

## Challenge #1: Longer Lifespans

On average, men and women who reach age 65 can expect to live well into their 80s. As you get older, naturally your life expectancy becomes longer.

As life expectancy continues to rise, the number of older people

29 Retirement Confidence Survey, 2025, EBRI, page 5, https://www.ebri.org/content/full/2025-ebri-greenwald-retirement-confidence-survey Accessed 8/11/2025.

in the United States is also growing. Projections show that by 2034, the number of adults aged 65 and older will outnumber those under 18, and by 2040, the older adult population is expected to swell to 80 million—up from 55.7 million in 2020.[30] Notably, the segment of adults aged 85 and older, who typically need more support, is projected to double by 2040.

Planning for a retirement that could last 20 or even 30 years—almost as long as someone's working life—is a major challenge. Retirement plans must take longer lifespans into account which bring on more challenges than the modern retiree's parents and grandparents faced. This means retirees will need to plan for more income and consider the possibility of needing expensive healthcare as they get older.

Many people also worry about making their savings last throughout retirement. In a 2025 survey, only two-thirds of workers were confident they knew how much income to withdraw from their savings and investments in retirement.[31] While the fear of running out of money is common, there are many strategies retirees can use to make sure their savings last.

---

***Fast Fact**: Health problems, caring for family, and lack of work contributed to the timing of retirement for 46% of retirees.*[32]

---

## Challenge #2: Retirement Date Timing

Traditionally, age 65 has been seen as the "normal" retirement age – after all, that's when Medicare kicks in, but many workers today end up retiring early. This is often due to health problems or company changes. Studies like the EBRI Retirement Confidence

30 Milken Institute. Innovative Financing and Care Models to Scale Affordable Housing Solutions for Middle-Income Older Adults. January 2024. https://milkeninstitute.org/content-hub/research-and-reports/reports/innovative-financing-and-care-models-scale-affordable-housing-solutions-middle-income-older-adults, Accessed 5/21/2025.
31 Retirement Confidence Survey, 2025, EBRI, page 13, https://www.ebri.org/content/full/2025-ebri-greenwald-retirement-confidence-survey Accessed 8/11/2025.
32 Retirement Confidence Survey, 2025, EBRI, page 13, https://www.ebri.org/content/full/2025-ebri-greenwald-retirement-confidence-survey Accessed 8/11/2025.

survey consistently find a sizable gap between workers' expected retirement age and their actual age of retirement.

For example, in 2024, 23 percent of workers said they planned to work until age 70. Or, like my father said, "I will work forever," not retiring at all. In reality, only six percent of retirees reported this was the case for them.[33]

Another important change is that retirement doesn't always mean stopping work completely. Many people today, who are healthier and live longer than retirees from previous generations, continue to work. In fact, 75 percent of retirees expect to work for pay during retirement.[34] This can mean that a modern retiree will have two or more retirements – first from their original career, and the second from their subsequent jobs.

The most common reasons for delaying retirement are:

- Not having enough savings.
- Increased cost of living.
- Fear of having to make substantial cuts to their spending due to these factors in retirement.[35]

While working during retirement is one way to allay these concerns, studies find a significant difference between a workers' plans and their actual experience once they do retire. Despite best-laid plans, our health and our bodies often have other ideas, which may be why only 29 percent of retirees report actually working for pay once retired.[36]

Some people keep working because they enjoy their jobs, while others switch to part-time work or start their own businesses. I speak with many people who want to continue to work because they want to stay socially connected and stay active both mentally and physically. Whatever your reasons for doing it, one thing is certain: continued good health remains key.

---

33 Retirement Confidence Survey, 2024 RCS FACT SHEET #2 EXPECTATIONS ABOUT RETIREMENT, https://www.ebri.org/docs/default-source/rcs/2024-rcs/rcs_24-fs-2.pdf?sfvrsn=2647072f_1 Accessed 8/26/2025.

34 Retirement Confidence Survey, 2025, EBRI, page 7, https://www.ebri.org/content/full/2025-ebri-greenwald-retirement-confidence-survey Accessed 8/11/2025.

35 Ibid.

36 Retirement Confidence Survey, 2025, EBRI, page 7, https://www.ebri.org/content/full/2025-ebri-greenwald-retirement-confidence-survey Accessed 8/11/2025.

***Fast Fact:*** *Only 15% of workers have access to a pension, according to Bureau of Labor Statistics data.*[37]

## Challenge #3: Decline in Company Pensions

Retirement planning used to be thought of as a three-legged stool. The first leg was Social Security, the second leg was a pension, and the third leg was your personal retirement savings. From these three legs, an employee could expect to replace most of their working income.

However, since the advent of the 401(k) plan in 1978, pensions have been going the way of the dinosaurs – extinct. Unless you work for the railroad, the government, or a school, you will most likely not receive a substantial pension. Pensions were a benefit that guaranteed lifelong income payments for as long as the worker was alive. They would typically increase as the salary increased and the longer the employee was with the company, so the employee pension would typically grow substantially in the final five to 10 years of employment.

Between the pension and Social Security, an average employee could have expected about 60 to 70 percent of their income to be replaced. There are many reasons why companies have shifted away from pensions. They were often costly and complicated to administer, required recalculating annual contributions each time they were made, and carried compliance and reporting obligations that were much more expensive than those associated with 401(k) plans.

The modern employer retirement account (401k/403b/457/TSP/etc.) shifts the risk and uncertainty of retirement income *to the employee*. The employee doesn't know exactly how much income they will be able to receive, and they must also control

37 Hartman, Rachel, and Brandon, Emily, 9 Jobs That Still Offer Traditional Pensions, U.S. News, Jan 2024, https://money.usnews.com/money/retirement/baby-boomers/articles/jobs-that-still-offer-traditional-pensions Accessed 2/3/2025.

the investments themselves along the way to retirement. Once you do retire, that's when the biggest change occurs: when you must now shift your saving and growing to saving and spending, but how do you take the income without running out of money? Figuring that out is also up to the employee.

---

***Fast Fact:*** *Social Security replaces about 40% of the average worker's income, yet experts suggest you will need 70% to 85% or morc to live comfortably in retirement.*[38]

---

## Challenge #4: Social Security

While almost everyone who works or is self-employed gets Social Security benefits when they retire, these benefits alone will not usually be enough to support a comfortable retirement. Generally, Social Security only replaces around 40 percent of the income for an average earner at age 65.

As the modern retiree moves from paying taxes to collecting benefits, the Social Security system is expected to face more pressure. The cost to keep the program running will increase substantially. According to the 2025 report from the Social Security and Medicare Boards of Trustees, starting in 2033, Social Security may not be able to pay full benefits to people who depend on it, with projected cuts of about 20 percent of benefits.[39]

To address these issues, Congress has already increased the age at which workers can receive full benefits. Other changes are likely, such as higher payroll taxes, lower benefits, changes to cost-of-living increases, or even privatizing some accounts. As of the writing of this book, the future changes of Social Security are unclear.

38 Social Security Administration, Understanding the Benefits, 2024, https://www.ssa.gov/pubs/EN-05-10024.pdf Accessed 1/10/2024.
39 Social Security, Detailed reports on the financial outlook for Social Security's Old-Age, Survivors, and Disability Insurance (OASDI) Trust Funds, 2025 Report, https://www.ssa.gov/oact/TR/ Accessed 8/26/2025.

What's clear is that the traditional retirement model, which relied heavily on employer and government support, is changing. Today, people are expected to take more responsibility for their own financial future. This means focusing on saving, investing wisely, and making sure assets are distributed in a way that helps meet retirement goals in a tax-efficient manner.

---

***Fast Fact:*** *The cost of healthcare is historically one of the highest-inflated products in the market.*[40]

---

## Challenge #5: Healthcare

Many employers offer group health insurance as a benefit to their employees, and some even extend this benefit to retirees. However, the cost of providing health insurance for retirees has risen in recent years. Because of this, some employers have passed on part of these increased costs to retirees by raising premiums, deductibles, or copayments. Others have reduced benefits or stopped offering retiree health coverage entirely.

As health care costs continue to go up, it is likely that many employers will keep cutting back or even eliminate health benefits for retirees. Retirees can buy health insurance on their own, either through individual plans for those under 65 or through Medicare supplement plans for those 65 and older. However, individually purchased health insurance can be very expensive.

- For people who are already retired, their greatest worry is the serious illness of a loved one.[41]
- According to the 2025 Fidelity Retiree Health Care Cost Estimate, a 65-year-old individual may need $172,500 in after-tax savings to cover health care

40 Rakshit, Shameek, et al, How does medical inflation compare to inflation in the rest of the economy? Peterson-KFF, Aug 2024, https://www.healthsystemtracker.org/brief/how-does-medical-inflation-compare-to-inflation-in-the-rest-of-the-economy/ Accessed 8/26/2025.

41 Senior Living, Top 10 Fears of Older Adults in 2024, https://www.seniorliving.org/finance/senior-fears-study/ Accessed 1/23/2024.

expenses in retirement.[42]

Because health care will likely be one of the largest expenses in retirement, retirees need to plan carefully for these costs.

---

***Fast Fact:*** *Only one in four American workers feel very confident about their ability to afford a comfortable retirement.*[43]

---

## Conclusion

Many older workers who have saved for retirement don't fully understand the options they have for taking money out of their retirement plans or the tax effects of these withdrawals. In fact, many people don't know what type of retirement plan they have, and most don't know the earliest age they can start receiving benefits or how taking benefits early affects the amount they receive.

This gap in knowledge highlights the importance of seeking sound financial advice so you can better understand your options, not only for withdrawing money from retirement accounts, but also how taxes may impact the income you'll have to live on in retirement. You might even find out that you have access to the funds without penalty earlier than you expected!

42 Fidelity Newsroom, Fidelity Investments® Releases 2025 Retiree Health Care Cost Estimate, a Timely Reminder for All Generations to Begin Planning, July 2025, https://newsroom.fidelity.com/pressreleases/fidelity-investments--releases-2025-retiree-health-care-cost-estimate--a-timely-reminder-for-all-gen/s/3c62e988-12e2-4dc8-afb4-f44b06c6d52e Accessed 9/02/2025.

43 Employee Benefit Research Institute and Greenwald Research. 2025 Retirement Confidence Survey. 2025. https://www.ebri.org/docs/default-source/rcs/2025-rcs/rcs_25-fs-3_prep.pdf?sfvrsn=f6e3042f_2, Accessed 5/21/2025.

## CHAPTER THREE CHALLENGE:

When do you think you will be *able to* retire?

________________________________________

________________________________________

________________________________________

________________________________________

When do you *want to* retire?

________________________________________

________________________________________

________________________________________

________________________________________

How long do you think that you will live? How confident are you in that number? Why?

________________________________________

________________________________________

________________________________________

________________________________________

To discuss the challenges that are preventing you from enjoying retirement, we invite you to schedule a complimentary interview by reaching out to us in one of three ways:

- By phone: (636) 388-7722
- By email: Info@RetirementWealthDesign.com
- Visit our website at: RetirementWealthDesign.com

# CHAPTER FOUR

## SEVEN STEPS TO SECURING AN INCOME

*"You must convert wealth into income at retirement."*
*~ Moshe A. Milevsky, PhD*

Many questions will come up as you get ready to retire. For example, how can I make the most money during retirement? What options do I have for taking money out of my IRAs and other retirement plans? And, most importantly, do I have "enough" to ensure my savings last throughout my entire retirement?

One of the most crucial parts of retirement planning is understanding how much wealth is actually "enough." This is a subjective determination, and the answer depends on both your financial resources and your personal goals for retirement.

The concept of "enough" is deeply tied to lifestyle choices. For some individuals, achieving financial independence with a moderate retirement lifestyle might be "enough." For others, the goal may be a more luxurious retirement with the freedom to travel, indulge in hobbies, and leave a significant legacy. To determine how much is enough, you must assess your personal values and desired experiences, taking into account your level of comfort and security.

What follows are the seven essential steps to take when deciding if you have enough to get a secure retirement income in place.

*__Fast Fact:__ Almost half of all retirees find that their overall expenses were higher than expected.*[44]

## STEP#1: Develop a Spending Plan

How much do you want coming in every month? Often, I read that 70 to 80 percent of what you were making when you were working should be the goal for your retirement. However, that is extremely broad and when we are discussing whether you are going to run out of money, I would prefer to take a little more of a personalized approach.

One way to make it more exact is to complete a comprehensive budget worksheet where you total up all your bills, average food costs, clothing purchases over the last year, etc. until you have tried to capture everything. Even for folks who complete a budget worksheet, I typically recommend adding 10 to 20 percent to it because items fluctuate or are easily missed. Besides, most of the retirees that I work with aren't just looking to survive retirement, they want to thrive – meaning they typically spend a little more than when they were working because they are eating out more, spending more on hobbies, seeing friends, or just having more experiences – which all cost money. Often the only major expense that I see decrease in retirement is fuel costs and auto maintenance.

So, what's another way? A shortcut approach is to look at your take home paycheck from your employer. After everything comes out – medical, dental, HSA, FICA, 401(k), etc. – what is the after-tax amount that hits your bank account?

Let's say it is $5,000 for example. You will then multiply that by how many paychecks that you receive each year (let's pretend it's bi-monthly, which is 24) so your take-home pay is $120,000 per year.

Now ask yourself, how much of your take-home pay are you saving outside of retirement accounts? Are you going into debt?

44 Retirement Confidence Survey, 2024, EBRI, https://www.ebri.org/docs/default-source/rcs/2024-rcs/2024-rcs-release-report.pdf?sfvrsn=2447072f_2 Page 10, Accessed 3/31/2025.

Or breaking even?

If you are saving, say you put $500 per paycheck into a brokerage account. That means your lifestyle expenses average $9,000 per month or $108,000 per year. So, if you want to retire and maintain your current lifestyle, then you will probably need about $108,000 per year coming in from your income sources. If this sounds like way too much or too little after you go through the exercise, then you'll have to complete a budget worksheet and match it up to your income.

Once you determine your lifestyle expenses, deduct major recurring payments that will end in retirement. Maybe you only have a year left to pay for your car and it is $1,000/month payment. We need to subtract that out and add in a future car payment for when you will need a new one. If you'll be paying off your house in retirement, we will need the mortgage payment to end up in your budget (keep the cost of taxes and insurance though). If you have credit card debt, student loan debt, or any other payments, you can line item those out for only the years that you will be paying them.

Liabilities (debt) can play an outsized role in retirement planning, especially if they involve long-term debt like mortgages or business loans. Understanding how much debt you carry, how long it will take to pay off, and the interest rates involved will affect both your monthly cash flow and your strategy for wealth preservation. It's important to distinguish between high-interest debt (credit cards, short-term loans) and lower-interest debt (mortgages or student loans), as your approach to managing them in retirement will vary.

Next, add additional expenses such as a potential kitchen remodel or a new home purchase. Maybe you want a travel plan of $10,000 per year for the first 15 years of retirement or to join a country club and play golf most days. We want to add these additional expenses because they will make a big impact and are higher dollar figures. Don't forget the car. You probably don't want to be 80 years old driving a 20-year-old car around. If it is unreliable, it might not be safe for you, so you will most likely need a new car at some point.

Healthcare is also a major expense in retirement that is often overlooked. If you retire before Medicare kicks in, you can estimate your healthcare costs until Medicare. When estimating Medicare costs, include the average cost of supplements, co-pays, and covered and non-covered prescriptions. It will vary depending on the person because of health status, but the average married couple enrolling in Medicare at age 65 can expect to spend upwards of $395,000 on these items in their lifetime.[45]

| | | MONTHLY | ANNUAL |
|---|---|---|---|
| **BASELINE** | Take Home Pay | $ 10,000 | $ 120,000 |
| | Savings from Take Home Pay | $ (1,000) | $ (12,000) |
| | | | |
| | | | |
| **DEBTS PAID OFF BY RETIREMENT** | | | |
| | Automobile | $ (1,000) | $ (12,000) |
| | Mortgage (Principal & Interest Only) | $ (2,000) | $ (24,000) |
| | | | |
| **ADDITIONAL RETIREMENT EXPENSES** | | | |
| | Travel | $ 833 | $ 10,000 |
| | Club Membership | $ 1,000 | $ 12,000 |
| | Medicare | $ 1,042 | $ 12,501 |
| | | | |
| **RETIREMENT INCOME TARGET (AFTER-TAX)** | | **$ 8,875** | **$ 106,501** |

Source: Author's own calculations.

The impact of inflation is particularly important when you're calculating retirement needs. Over time, rising costs will affect your purchasing power, so you'll need to estimate your future expenses in today's dollars while factoring in inflation. A reasonable assumption is to project inflation at three percent annually, though it can be higher depending on economic conditions. In the U.S., it has averaged 3.3 percent for the last 100 years, however the last 20 years has seen significant variations, averaging roughly 2.3 to 2.7 percent annually.[46]

Additionally, your plan must account for the possibility of living

45 Godbout, Ted, Here's How Much Retirees May Need for Healthcare Costs, NAPA, July 2025, https://www.napa-net.org/news/2024/7/heres-how-much-retirees-may-need-healthcare-costs/ Accessed 9/02/2025.

46 US Inflation Calculator, Current US Inflation Rates: 2000-2025, https://www.usinflationcalculator.com/inflation/current-inflation-rates/ Accessed 9/02/2025.

longer than expected. With people living longer than ever before, it's critical to plan for at least 20 years of retirement, especially as healthcare improves and life expectancy rises. This means your retirement income needs to cover a potentially lengthy period of time—more than one might initially assume.

---

***Fast Fact:*** *Americans frequently fail to understand their own life expectancy and the financial implications of a longer retirement.*[47]

---

## STEP#2: Identify Income Sources

It would be pretty tough to win a baseball game if you didn't know the order that you should run the bases. Although, when I coached little league, we still found a way....sometimes.

The next step in your process is going to be to take an inventory of your financial assets. If you haven't already, visit ssa.gov to get your latest Social Security estimates. These will give you different ages at which you can take Social Security. List out your retirement plans and the amount in each one.

- Do you have IRAs, ROTH IRAs, HSAs, Brokerage accounts, CDs, Treasuries, or Annuities?
- Where are they and can you get a statement or online access?
- Do you have checking and savings accounts, and how much is in them? Some modern retirees own real estate interests; if you do - how much are they worth, how much do you owe, what is your profit, and what is your plan with them in retirement?
- Do you have a pension – how much will it be and what are your options? Does it increase with inflation or remain level?

---

47 TIAA Institute, New Study Finds One in Four Millennial U.S. Workers Expect to Live 30 or More Years in Retirement, April 2025, https://www.tiaa.org/public/institute/about/news/millennial-workers-years-in-retirement Accessed 9/02/2025.

As we put a strategic income plan together, we need to have all your financial pieces on the table so we can determine the most efficient order to take them in and how to stack or invest them based on your timeline. They are all important and all have a role to play in your retirement approach. There is no insignificant asset or liability.

The shift from wealth building (accumulation) to taking an income from your savings (distribution) is one of the most vital shifts that a worker will make in their life. The rules shift, how you invest becomes even more important, and the order in which you take your money could mean the difference between leaving a legacy and running out of money. We will discuss the investment strategies in future chapters, but for this chapter, we will continue to focus on strategies to take income.

---

***Fast Fact:*** *Social Security replaces about 40% of the average worker's income, and experts suggest you will need 70% to 85% or more of earnings to live comfortably in retirement.*[48]

---

## STEP#3: Strategies for Where and When to Take the Income

During retirement, the main priority is to ensure your savings will last and to manage your money to meet your needs. The order in which you take money out from different accounts can have a big impact on financial security for the rest of your life. These are some common strategies to use for withdrawing money.

### *The 4 Percent Rule Strategy*

The 4 percent rule is likely the most referenced and sited retirement withdrawal rule in the industry and has gained widespread recognition as a reliable method for determining

48 Social Security Administration, Understanding the Benefits, 2024, https://www.ssa.gov/pubs/EN-05-10024.pdf Accessed 1/10/2024.

sustainable withdrawal rates. In fact, if you were to search on the internet "safe withdrawal rate in retirement" this is often the first item that pops up. Because of its popularity, I will dive into the origins, methodology, benefits, and criticisms of the 4 percent rule, offering insights into its application in retirement planning.

The 4 percent rule was first introduced by financial planner William Bengen in a landmark study published in 1994. Bengen sought to determine the maximum withdrawal rate that would allow retirees to sustain their portfolios for at least 30 years under varying market conditions. By analyzing historical data on stock and bond returns, Bengen concluded that retirees could withdraw 4 percent of their initial portfolio value in the first year of retirement and adjust subsequent withdrawals for inflation, without running out of money in most scenarios. This approach became widely known as the *4 Percent Rule*.

The 4 percent rule is based on a simple framework:

1. **Initial Withdrawal:** In the first year of retirement, the retiree withdraws 4 percent of their portfolio's starting value. For example, a retiree with a $1,000,000 portfolio would withdraw $40,000.
2. **Inflation Adjustment:** Each year thereafter, the withdrawal amount is adjusted to account for inflation, ensuring the retiree's purchasing power remains consistent.
3. **Portfolio Composition:** The rule assumes a portfolio with a balanced allocation of stocks and bonds, typically a 50 to 75 percent allocation to equities and the remainder in fixed-income securities.

*Example Calculation:* Consider a retiree with a $500,000 portfolio.

- Year 1: Withdraws 4 percent, or $20,000.
- Year 2: If inflation is 2 percent, the withdrawal increases to $20,400.
- Year 3: If inflation is 3 percent, the withdrawal rises to $21,012.

This process continues annually, allowing the retiree to maintain a steady standard of living.

The advantages of the 4 percent rule are three-fold. First, is its simplicity because it provides a straightforward and easily implementable strategy for retirees. Second, at the time it was published, it was historically reliable because Bengen's research demonstrated that the 4 percent rule worked across numerous market conditions, including the Great Depression and high-inflation periods. Lastly, it allowed for inflation protection by adjusting the withdrawals for inflation. The rule helps ensure that retirees maintain their purchasing power over time.

Despite its popularity, the 4 percent rule is not without its critics. Some of the primary concerns include:

1. **Changing Market Conditions:** Critics argue that historical data may not accurately reflect future market performance, particularly in an era of lower expected returns on stocks and bonds.
2. **Rigid Framework:** The rule does not account for individual variations, such as differing spending needs, health expenses, or unexpected financial shocks.
3. **Sequence of Returns Risk:** Retirees who experience significant market declines early in retirement may find their portfolios depleted faster than anticipated.
4. **Tax Implications:** The rule assumes withdrawals are made from a tax-deferred account, but tax obligations can vary significantly based on the retiree's financial situation.

To address these criticisms, some financial planners have proposed several adaptations to the 4 percent rule:

1. **Dynamic Withdrawals:** Adjust withdrawals based on portfolio performance, increasing them in strong market years and reducing them during downturns.
2. **Guardrails Strategy:** Set upper and lower limits on withdrawal rates to prevent over- or under-spending.
3. **Variable Withdrawal Rates:** Use a higher or lower initial withdrawal rate based on market conditions at retirement.

Additionally, other methods like the *Bucket Strategy* or using annuities can complement or replace the 4 percent rule, depending on individual needs.

***The Bucket Strategy***

Another way to manage your withdrawals is by using the bucket strategy. This approach divides your savings into different "buckets" based on how long you expect to need the money and the level of risk you're willing to take. Each bucket is filled with investments that match its time horizon and risk level:

- **Bucket #1:** This is the money you'll use in the first one to three years of retirement. It includes low risk, liquid investments like CDs, money markets, and short-term treasuries.
- **Bucket #2:** This bucket is for the next three to five-10 years. It has slightly higher risk investments, like short-term bond funds or indexed annuities.
- **Buckets #3 and #4:** These buckets are for the long term (10-20+ years). They contain more aggressive investments, like mutual funds and stocks. When Bucket #1 is used up, you can move money from Bucket #2 to refill it and move money from Bucket #3 to refill Bucket #2, and so on.

This strategy is more advanced than just withdrawing a set percentage each year. It needs to be adjusted based on your income needs, risk tolerance, and the performance of your investments.

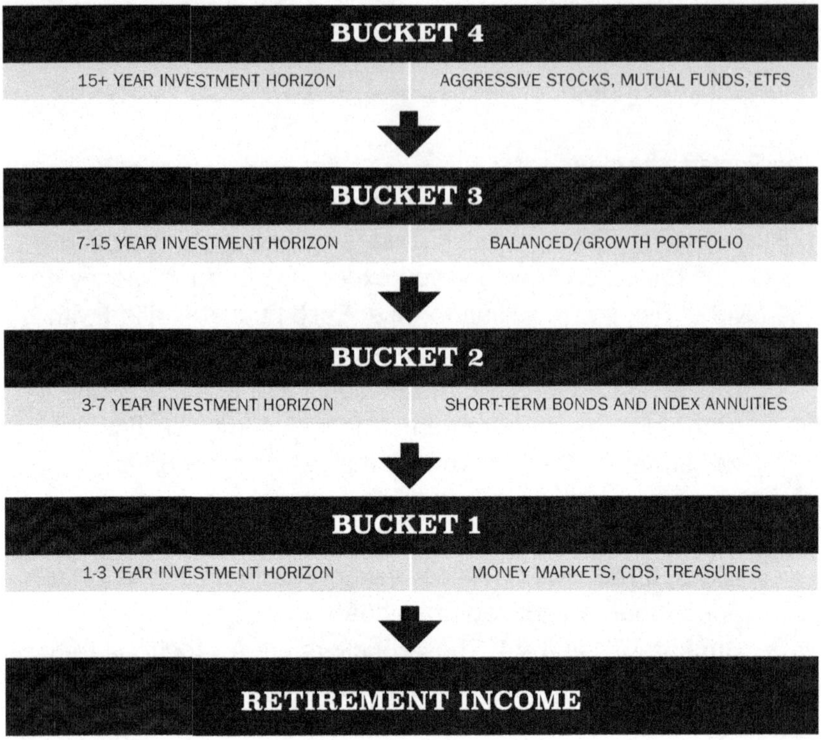


Source: Author's own calculations.

***The Personal Pension Strategy***

Whether you have a current pension or not, many people like the simplicity that a pension provides and prefer a straightforward income plan without too many moving parts. They want to create a fixed income source that they cannot outlive to provide guaranteed income for the rest of their lives (if married, the spouse included).

The goal of the strategy is to use only a portion of your retirement savings, in combination with Social Security, real estate income flows (if applicable), and any other pensions (if applicable), to create a monthly income that will meet your living needs for the rest of your life. Typically, an **annuity** is used to create personal pension, however, we will discuss the types of annuities and pros/cons in future chapters.

In order to establish this strategy, we create just two buckets:

- **"Needs/Income" Bucket:** The total monthly income from this bucket should meet your daily living expenses for the rest of your life. The sources of these funds should be fixed for the rest of your life such as from social security, pensions, and annuities.
- **"Fun/Flexible/Future" Bucket:** These are the funds that are left over after the first bucket is filled. These funds could be depleted, and you would still receive the "Needs/Income" for the rest of your life, providing income security in case you live a long time. These funds can be flexible – maybe you want to travel more and take more out in the early years of retirement and less in later years – and should be invested or withdrawn based on your financial/lifestyle goals other than just living expenses. Or these funds can be saved for a future date, whether they are needed for future healthcare should you become sick, or if you would like to grow your legacy.

| NEEDS | FUN |
|---|---|
| Guaranteed Income for life, no matter how long you live | Stocks, Bonds, Mutual Funds, ETFs |
| Should cover basic living needs to ensure you "don't run out of money" | Flexible withdrawals as wanted |
| | This money will be for your other financial goals outside of just living expenses |

Source: Author's own calculations.

An example of this strategy might look like this:

- John and Jane Doe would like to have $7,500 per month (after-tax) of income coming in for retirement for their living expenses. All of their retirement savings are in pre-tax 401(k)s, so the estimated before tax income amount they will need is $9,250 to cover state and federal taxes.
- Social Security will total $6,500 per month combined for them at retirement, which they are planning on taking when they retire. This means that their income gap is $2,750 per month ($9,250 - $6,500 = $2,750).
- They decide to use the personal pension strategy. Of their $1,000,000 saved, they move $600,000 of their savings into an annuity that will provide $2,750 of monthly income for the rest of their lives, no matter how long either of them lives. This annuity has provisions that will allow it to increase payment amounts as the stock market rises in the future. This would combat inflation, and if they pass away prematurely, the remaining balance of their account will go to their children.
- They now have their "living expense needs" guaranteed for the rest of their lives by only using 60 percent of their household retirement savings. This then leaves 40 percent ($400,000) invested to grow in the market for future use on vacations, remodeling the house, and leaving to their children.

| NEEDS | | FUN | |
|---|---|---|---|
| SOURCE | GUARANTEED MONTHLY INCOME (+INFLATION) | SOURCE | WITHDRAWALS AS NEEDED/ WANTED |
| SOCIAL SECURITY | $ 6,500 | IRA / 401(k) | $ 400,000 |
| ANNUITY | $ 2,750 | | |

Source: Author's own calculations.

## STEP#4: Consider Taxes and Asset Withdrawal

When it comes to withdrawing money, the goal is to minimize taxes. You'll typically have three types of investment accounts to pull income from:

- **Taxable investments:** These include savings accounts, corporate bonds, money market accounts, brokerage accounts, certificates of deposits (CDs) and mutual funds. They are taxed at ordinary income rates or capital gains rates (depending on how long you've held them). Generally, capital gains rates are lower than ordinary income rates, but they can change.
- **Tax-deferred investments:** This includes things like 401(k) s, 403(b)s, 457s, SIMPLE IRAs, TSP, traditional IRAs, and annuities. You don't pay taxes on these until you withdraw the money.
- **Tax-free investments:** These include Roth IRAs, Roth 401(k)s, ROTH TSP, and some cash-value life insurance. You don't pay taxes on these when you withdraw them.

Each type of investment is taxed differently. The goal is to figure out how to use your savings in a way that minimizes taxes and helps your money last longer.

**A common strategy is to:**

1. Withdraw from taxable accounts first.
2. Withdraw from tax-deferred accounts next (like traditional IRAs and 401(k)s).
3. Withdraw from tax-free accounts last (like Roth IRAs).

With this strategy, your tax-deferred and tax-free accounts grow as long as possible and you avoid paying taxes on them early. In addition, drawing from taxable accounts first can help reduce the taxes you pay on income later in retirement.

After you've withdrawn from taxable accounts, you can start using your tax-deferred accounts like traditional IRAs and 401(k)

s. By waiting to use these accounts, your savings have had more time to grow without being taxed. However, be aware that you'll need to start taking **required minimum distributions (RMDs)** from traditional IRAs at age 73/75, or from 401(k)s at the later of age 73/75, or retirement.

Tax-free accounts, like Roth IRAs, are usually the last to be used. Distributions from Roth IRAs are tax-free if you're at least 59½ years old and have had the account for at least five years. You don't have to worry about RMDs with Roth IRAs during your lifetime, but your heirs will need to withdraw the funds within 10 years of your death (unless they're eligible for lifetime withdrawals). By leaving tax-free accounts to grow, you can avoid paying taxes on your savings, giving you more flexibility and tax benefits in the long run.

***Case Study: Paying NO Taxes on $100,000 of Annual Retirement Income***

Most retirees assume they'll pay less in taxes once they stop working—but that isn't always the case. Required Minimum Distributions (RMDs), Social Security taxes, and capital gains can create a nasty surprise. But with the right strategy, you can dramatically reduce your tax bill in retirement.

Let's look at a real-world inspired case study. Bob and Susan, age 67 and 66, have the following income in retirement:

- $60,000/year in combined Social Security benefits
- $700,000 in Traditional IRAs
- $250,000 in a joint brokerage account
- $50,000 in cash savings

Their goal? *Generate $100,000 in annual income while minimizing taxes.*

**The Strategy:** Instead of pulling the entire $40,000 difference from their IRA (which would be fully taxable and trigger additional taxes on social security), Bob and Susan take a multi-source income approach:

- $60,000 from Social Security

- $21,500 from their joint brokerage account ($5,000 long-term capital gains)
- $18,500 from their Traditional IRA

Here's why this works so well:

1. **Social Security Taxation is Tiered:** Only $14,075 of their Social Security is taxable because their other income is strategically kept low.
2. **Capital Gains Are Favorably Taxed:** Long-term capital gains from the brokerage account can be taxed at 0 percent if their taxable income stays below certain thresholds.
3. **IRA Withdrawals Fill the Lower Brackets:** The $18,500 IRA withdrawal keeps them in the 12 percent marginal bracket. This, combined with their taxable Social Security, falls under the standard deduction, eliminating income tax.
4. **Cash Provides Flexibility:** In future years, they can use cash savings or adjust withdrawal sources to manage RMDs and avoid bumping into higher Medicare premiums (IRMAA).

**The Result:** With this blend of income sources, Bob and Susan take home nearly all of their $100,000. Their total federal income tax bill? $0. No IRMAA surcharges. No surprises.

**The Consideration:** This was Bob and Susan's goal: to pay 0 percent taxes. We did consider and discuss the impact of ROTH Conversions and the benefits the ROTH Conversion could have on their future tax savings once required minimum distributions began. We measured the tax impact of bumping their IRA distribution up to $79,000 which would take them to the top of the 12 percent tax bracket, causing their effective tax rate to increase from 0 percent to 11.94 percent ($17,193.51 in taxes) but would shelter $43,306 in a Roth IRA. After we ran the math, they made the educated decision to not perform the ROTH conversion.

**What This Means for You:** This kind of result doesn't happen by accident. It takes coordination between Social Security, IRA withdrawals, and taxable account strategies. Every couple's plan will be different—but smart tax planning can help you keep more of what you've earned.

---

***Fast Fact:*** *Americans who work with a financial advisor expect to retire two years sooner than those who don't work with an advisor.*[49]

---

## STEP#5: Assess Early Retirement

If you choose to retire before age 59½, there are additional withdrawal options that may be available to you. Retiring early adds complexity to your income plan but can be easily achieved with proactive structuring of your investments and income distributions. Often times people that want to retire before 59½ AND have the ability to, are hesitant because they are afraid of the penalties that they will face when trying to access their retirement funds.

Generally speaking, retirement accounts cannot be accessed without a 10 percent penalty until age 59½ There are two rules, however, that might allow access to these funds early.

- The Rule of 55 is a guideline that allows people aged 55 or older to withdraw money from their 401(k) or 403(b) retirement accounts without paying the usual 10 percent early withdrawal penalty. This rule applies if you leave your job during or after the year you turn 55. Not all plans have adopted this rule, so it is important to ask your plan administrator.
- The 72(t) Rule is a tax provision that allows people to take early withdrawals from their retirement accounts, like an IRA, without paying the usual 10 percent penalty, even if you are under age 59½. To use this rule, you must take regular, equal payments for at least five years or until you turn

---

49 Northwestern Mutual, Planning & Progress Study, 2024, Value of an Advisor, https://news.northwesternmutual.com/planning-and-progress-study-2024 Accessed 1/23/2025.

59½, whichever is longer. It's a useful option for those who need access to their savings early, but it requires careful planning to avoid penalties or financial shortfalls.

Access to healthcare is also a major consideration with early retirement. We will discuss healthcare in future chapters, but there are many options available. In my opinion, a person shouldn't wait to retire just because Medicare does not kick in until age 65. If your spending and income plans account for healthcare costs—and your income will last—you have the option to retire.

From a planning perspective, a major consideration during this process is where your income will come from in regard to the tax treatment. Because if you are using the ACA Marketplace to get your healthcare, there can be significant subsidies given, making it very affordable if your taxable income is low enough. This would mean that we would draw your income in the early years from accounts other than the pre-tax type of retirement accounts.

---

***Fast Fact:*** *Nearly 80% of people nearing retirement don't have a basic knowledge of Social Security retirement benefits.*[50]

---

## STEP#6: Customize Your Social Security

For most Americans, you have paid into Social Security your entire working career, and you'll receive the payouts from it during your retirement. There are numerous resources for Social Security rules, but for the modern retiree, they are more concerned with when to take it.

Depending on what you read or who you speak with, often the advice seems one sided – always take it early or always take it late. Because of rule changes over the years, those are your

50 Feldman, Jamie. "Nearly Half of Americans Failed This Social Security Quiz About Retirement." Kiplinger, March 2024, https://www.kiplinger.com/retirement/social-security/many-americans-failed-this-social-security-quiz, Accessed 6/10/2025.

main options. I believe the strategy that you use to take Social Security very much depends on your personal retirement plan. For the purposes of this book, I am going to focus on many of the situations and considerations that I encounter and will reference the rules of Social Security that are in place at the time of this writing.

Social Security benefits are calculated based on how much you earned during your working years and how long you worked. The **Social Security Administration (SSA)** looks at your highest 35 years of earnings, adjusts those amounts for inflation, and averages them. This average is called your Average Indexed Monthly Earnings (AIME). Then, they use a formula to calculate your Primary Insurance Amount (PIA), which is the base amount you'll receive if you start benefits at your **full retirement age (FRA)**. The formula is designed so people with lower earnings get a higher percentage of their income replaced than people with higher earnings. Each person's Social Security benefits are specific to them, so please visit ssa.gov in order to see your projected benefits.

Unless you are a widow or are disabled, the minimum age that you can take Social Security is 62. If you were born in the year 1960 or later, your full retirement age is 67 years old. Each month before your FRA that you take Social Security, your benefit is reduced so the longer that you wait to take it, the more that it grows. Between FRA and 70 years old, it grows at a higher rate than it did before FRA.

## Projected Benefits Based on a $2,000 Income at Full Retirement Age

| AGE | BENEFIT % | BENEFIT $ |
|---|---|---|
| | Actuarial Reduction | |
| 62 | 70% | $1,750 |
| 63 | 75% | $1,875 |
| 64 | 80% | $2,000 |
| 65 | 86.7% | $2,167 |
| 66 | 93.3% | $2,333 |
| | Full Retirement Age | |
| 67 | 100% | $2,500 |
| | Delayed Retirement Credits | |
| 68 | 108% | $2,700 |
| 69 | 116% | $2,900 |
| 70 | 124% | $3,100 |

Source: Savvy Social Security

If you decide to take Social Security before your FRA and you continue to work or work part-time, there is a limit to how much you can make in *working* income before you get a reduction in benefits.[51] Keep in mind that this is only applicable to working or earned income and does not apply to distributions from retirement accounts or passive income.

For 2025, if you were below full retirement age for the entire year, you could have earned up to $23,400 without any reduction in benefits.[52] Earnings above this threshold resulted in a reduction of $1 in benefits for every $2 earned over the limit. If you reached full retirement age in 2025, a higher earnings limit applied. In this case, you could have earned up to $62,160 in the

51 Social Security Administration, Receiving Benefits While Working, 2025, https://www.ssa.gov/benefits/retirement/planner/whileworking.html Accessed 9/02/2025.
52 Ibid

months before reaching full retirement age without a reduction in benefits. Earnings exceeding this amount led to a reduction of $1 in benefits for every $3 earned over the limit.

It's important to note that these reductions are temporary. Once you reach full retirement age, your monthly benefit will be adjusted to account for the months in which benefits were withheld due to excess earnings. This means you can recoup the withheld amounts over time. Additionally, the earnings limits are adjusted annually to account for changes in average wages, so it's advisable to check the current limits each year.

Once you reach FRA, you can earn as much money from work as you would like and collect Social Security without any reduction in benefits. The downside to doing this, though, is that you could be in a higher tax bracket and your Social Security benefit is likely to be taxed at that level. Taxes on Social Security will be discussed in a later chapter.

So, if you plan to work in retirement, it is important to consider the impact that it will have on your Social Security benefit if you elect to take it early.

---

***Fast Fact:*** *In 2024, about 68 million Americans will receive over $1.5 trillion in Social Security benefits paid during the year.*[53]

---

Many people that I come across discuss the "break-even" age of Social Security. This is the point when the higher monthly benefits catch up to the total amount that you would have received by starting earlier. For most people, this happens around age 78-82, depending on benefit amount and lifespan. If you live past your break-even age, delaying benefits could lead to a higher lifetime payout.

53 Social Security Administration Fact Sheet, 2024, https://www.ssa.gov/news/press/factsheets/basicfact-alt.pdf Accessed 1/10/2025.

However, I often point out that this calculation usually doesn't account for the potential growth of your investment accounts if you don't need to draw from them because of your Social Security income. It also doesn't take into account the cost-of-living adjustments (COLA) that Social Security often provides. So, the break-even point, although it is a data point, may not be the most accurate information to base your decision on when it comes to Social Security planning.

*Then what should we consider when taking Social Security?*

First would be health. If you are in good health and have longevity in your family, that is a major consideration to delay Social Security. Next would be your income plan. If you delay Social Security, will you be taking too much money out of your investments that any market risk would be catastrophic to your income plan? Would you have to invest so conservatively during this time that you might not get reasonable growth? Third would be your amount of liquid (accessible) savings. If you delay your Social Security, will you be spending through all of your accessible and flexible savings to the point that in the future you would be unable to fund an emergency that arises?

For married couples, spousal Social Security benefits let a husband or wife receive payments based on their spouse's work history instead of their own. These benefits are helpful if one spouse earned significantly less money during their working years or didn't work enough to qualify for Social Security on their own. If you qualify, you can get up to 50 percent of your spouse's full retirement benefit amount. You can start as early as age 62, but if you claim before your full retirement age (FRA), the amount will be smaller and to get the full 50 percent, you must wait until your FRA. You can't claim spousal benefits until your spouse starts receiving their own Social Security. Also, if you worked and earned Social Security benefits on your own, you'll receive the higher amount between your own benefit and the spousal benefit, but not both.

Lastly, *if one spouse passes away, the surviving spouse gets to keep the higher of the two amounts.* The reason this is important is that sometimes if you are married, it can make sense for one spouse to file and collect it early (typically the lower benefit recipient) and delay the higher earning spouse. What will happen when you do this is that you will receive some payments early on, then when the higher spouse collects, the lower earning spouse will get a bump up in benefit to their adjusted spousal level. Then if one spouse passes away, the surviving spouse still keeps the highest payment amount.

For example, let's say that the husband's FRA benefit will be $4,000 at age 67 when he retires. The wife's benefit (she is the same age as the husband) will receive her own Social Security benefit of $500 at age 62, and is already retired. If the wife begins collecting Social Security at age 62, the household will have $500 of extra income per month until age 67. Then, when the husband files at age 67, he will receive $4,000, and the wife's benefit will bump up to $1,400. And if the husband passes before his wife, the wife will get his $4,000 per month of benefit. This is not always the best strategy when married, however, it can be useful for some couples.

---

***Fast Fact:*** *Corporations faced with market volatility and geopolitical uncertainty generated a record-breaking 138 percent increase in pension buyout plans for 2023.*[54]

---

## STEP#7: Optimize Employer Pension Plans

There are not as many employer pension plans in existence today as there were previously, however there are some companies including the federal government that still have them for employees. Generally, the amount that a pension plan will pay is based on a flat or fixed dollar amount or a percentage of the employee's annual compensation.

54 LIMRA, LIMRA: New U.S. Pension Risk Transfer Sales Posts Double-Digit Growth in First Quarter 2023, May 2023, https://www.limra.com/en/newsroom/news-releases/2023/limra-new-u.s.-pension-risk-transfer-sales-posts-double-digit-growth-in-first-quarter-2023/ Accessed 1/18/2024.

The formula also typically includes a multiplying factor based on the years of service with the employer. Because the formula components are salary and years of service, most recipients of pensions see their payout amounts drastically increase during their final three to five years of service.

**The employer bears the weight of responsibilities with pensions**. These responsibilities include making regular contributions, investing the funds that will be used for future benefits, and supplementing them with additional contributions to keep it fully funded. Private sector pensions are insured by the Pension Benefit Guaranty Corporation (PBGC), which is a federal agency that will take over the plan if the pension plan becomes underfunded and in financial distress. When this happens, the PBGC only guarantees benefits up to certain limits set by the federal government.

Participants in pension plans will receive their full benefit when they reach "normal retirement age" which is typically 65, but will be defined by the plan. They typically allow participants to take early retirement benefits as well after satisfying a certain number of years. The best way to find out is to speak with your benefits department and request a pension benefits estimate for the ages that you are considering retiring.

Pensions will have defined rules for how they pay out. Here are the most common:

- **Straight Life Annuity:** The highest payment amount (i.e. $1,150) that is guaranteed for the life of the individual participant. When the participant dies, all payments stop.
- **Joint and 50 percent Survivor Annuity:** This will be a reduced initial payment (i.e. $1,000) and when the primary participant dies, the surviving spouse will receive 50 percent of the initial amount ($500). When the surviving spouse dies, all payments stop.
- **Joint and 100 percent Survivor Annuity:** This will reduce the initial payment (i.e. $950) and when the primary participant dies, the surviving spouse receives 100 percent of the initial amount (i.e. $950). When the surviving spouse

dies, all payments stop.

- **Life with 10-year Period Certain Annuity:** This will reduce the payment slightly (i.e. $1,100) and provide payments guaranteed for the life of the primary participant. If the primary participant dies within the first 10 years, the payment will continue to the beneficiary until a combined total of 10 years of payments have been made. Then all payments will end.
- **Lump Sum Withdrawal:** This option gives a dollar value that the participant will receive instead of taking the annuity payments. This gives participants the flexibility to invest according to their own preferences and ensures that the funds are held outside the company, rather than being tied to a company-funded pension plan. The participant can withdraw the funds personally, but then they will be taxed immediately on the entire lump sum distribution, OR they can rollover the funds to an IRA where they will not be taxed on the money until it is taken out.

How you choose to take your pension is an extremely important decision and should be made with significant consideration to how it will interact with the rest of your plan. I have some clients that the payout amount compared to the lump sum is extremely favorable, so it makes a lot of sense to take the annuity payouts. Others have pensions where the payout is so low that it makes sense to take the lump sum. I have some that are concerned with inflation and the pension payouts are not inflation adjusted, or they are concerned with leaving a legacy and would rather have the money rolled to an IRA so it can be inherited. I even have some clients that take the lump sum because they are worried about the sustainability of their former company and don't want the reduced payout from the PBGC if their former company can no longer keep the pension fully funded.

## Conclusion

You should not have a plan to retire without a *retirement income plan*. For the modern retiree, it is critical to know the rules and clarify how much money is coming from where and when. A solid income plan could mean either more income, more security, or more inheritance as compared to possibly running out of money. Understanding what you have available and how you can best utilize your savings will provide you clarity, which often gives you confidence and allows you to enjoy what you have worked so hard to achieve.

## CHAPTER FOUR CHALLENGE:

List your current income sources for retirement and when you plan to access them.

____________________________________________________

____________________________________________________

____________________________________________________

If you have a pension, how will you take it? Does it adjust for inflation?

____________________________________________________

____________________________________________________

____________________________________________________

When will you start Social Security? If you are married, when will your spouse start Social Security?

____________________________________________________

____________________________________________________

____________________________________________________

What healthcare coverage will you have in retirement? How much will it cost?

______________________________________________

______________________________________________

______________________________________________

How much do you plan to spend each month/year in retirement?

______________________________________________

______________________________________________

______________________________________________

List your investment accounts and the balances.

______________________________________________

______________________________________________

______________________________________________

List your cash savings accounts and amounts.

______________________________________________

______________________________________________

______________________________________________

List your rental properties and their worth, debt, profit, and plan.

______________________________________________

______________________________________________

______________________________________________

What income strategy do you prefer?
4 Percent / Buckets / Personal Pension / Other

______________________________________________

______________________________________________

How will you withdraw money based on the tax-treatment of the accounts?

______________________________________________

______________________________________________

______________________________________________

To schedule a complimentary review of your income plan or to discuss potential strategies that could boost your income and save you money, please reach out to us in one of three ways:

- By phone: (636) 388-7722
- By email: Info@RetirementWealthDesign.com
- Visit our website at: RetirementWealthDesign.com

# CHAPTER FIVE

## INVESTING WITH PURPOSE AND ON PURPOSE IN RETIREMENT

*"Efficiency is doing things right; effectiveness is doing the right things."*
*~ Peter F. Drucker*

Earlier this year in Missouri, we had 15-inches of snow fall in about 24 hours. For our area, that is pretty good snow. As the snow started to slow down and it looked like the storm was coming to an end, I put on my winter gear and headed out to start shoveling. I was feeling pretty good as I walked outside and looking around my street, I was the first one that was going to have a clean driveway. My mood quickly shifted as I realized this was going to take a while. Thirty minutes into shoveling, I felt defeated. I had made very little progress and started doing the math on how long this was going to take to finish.

At about that time, my neighbor comes walking across the street and says, "Tom, what are you doing?! You should've just asked to use my snowblower! I bought it just for this type of snow and I don't get to use it that often. Come on over and grab it, you'll be done twice as fast, and you'll save your back."

What a blessing! Using the snowblower was so much more efficient and it cut my time by more than half. On top of saving time, it made the job easier, look better, and I was in a much better mood as I was working through it. The funny thing was that before I began, I knew he had a snowblower because I had used it before, I just had some underlying belief that it might be inconvenient for him if I used it or might put him out in some way.

When it comes to investing for retirement, like the snowblower, sometimes there are much more efficient ways to get the job done that will save time, save stress, and help your retirement path look even better for you and your family.

Beliefs and behaviors in our investment philosophy often come from deep-seeded emotions tied to both conscious and subconscious memories of what we have heard and experienced in our past. Yes, emotions play a critical role in how you choose to invest, whether you are aware or unaware of them, whether you are active in the management of your investments or let someone else manage them, and whether you take a lot or a little risk.

I have had numerous conversations that had different details but sounded very similar. Often it goes like this, "I had an uncle who had worked hard his entire life, was great at what he did, and after saving for 40 years decided to retire. I watched him retire in 2007 and he was as happy as can be. Then in 2008 he lost everything. Half of his money was gone, and he had to go back to work. I don't want that to be me."

A Smart Asset study in 2025 found that, after accounting for inflation and fees, individuals who worked with an advisor earned an average rate of return that was two to three percent higher than individuals who did not work with an advisor.[55] Now of course not all financial advisors operate the same way or have similar returns, and the risk adjusted returns will vary, however this demonstrates there is value in using an advisor managed portfolio.

The reasons why they are better could vary. The logical answer might lean towards research, experience, and data analysis, however, multiple firms have published data demonstrating the emotional toll of self-managed investing on performance. The latest DALBAR Quantitative Analysis of Investor Behavior, for instance, found that the average equity fund investor earned

55 DeJohn, Jaclyn, The Value of a Financial Advisor: What's It Really Worth? Jan 2025, https://smartasset.com/financial-advisor/financial-advisor-value-model, Accessed 9/23/2025.

returns that were 8.66 percent *lower* compared to the S&P 500 index.[56]

Research demonstrates a common investment concept emphasizing the importance of staying invested in the stock market during the worst days to avoid missing its best days. Interestingly, these best days often occur during periods of high volatility or shortly after major downturns. Therefore, attempting to time the market by jumping in and out can be risky.

It can also be hard to stomach, especially during retirement when you're investing from a finite pot of funds, which is why emotions play no small part. Vanguard's new Emotional & Time Value Advice study found that 83 percent of investors reported having greater peace of mind related to their finances when working with an advisor.[57] Not only did they experience fewer negative and more positive emotions, but they reported saving time—over 100 hours annually—which allowed them to spend more time doing the things they enjoyed.[58]

Maintaining a consistent investment strategy, even during turbulent times, is generally advised to capture and enhance long-term returns. A bear market crash is a loss of at least 20 percent. During retirement, how many of these bear markets will you likely see?

There have been 15 bear markets since 1942 with an average loss of 31.7 percent and an average duration of 11.1 months.[59] That means that a market crash of at least 20 percent has occurred on average every 5.5 years! If you are planning on being retired for 25 years, that means that you can expect to have at least four market crashes during your retirement. With this being true, the best way to approach the problem is to be proactive

---

56 Dalbar, Inc. "2025 QAIB Press Release: Investor Behavior Studies Continue to Show Gap in Returns." QAIB Report, Dalbar, Inc. March 2025, https://www.dalbar.com/Portals/dalbar/Cache/News/PressReleases/2025QAIBPressRelease.pdf Accessed 9/22/2025.

57 Vanguard, Advice Pays in Peace of Mind and Time: Vanguard Survey Reveals Hidden Value of Financial Advice, July 2025, https://corporate.vanguard.com/content/corporatesite/us/en/corp/who-we-are/pressroom/press-release-advice-pays-in-peace-of-mind-and-time-vanguard-survey-reveals-hidden-value-of-financial-advice-07072025.html Accessed 9/23/2025.

58 Ibid.

59 First Trust, History of U.S. Bear & Bull Markets, March 2025, https://www.ftportfolios.com/COMMON/CONTENTFILELOADER.ASPX?CONTENTGUID=4ECFA978-D0BB-4924-92C8-628FF9BFE12D Accessed 9/23/2025.

instead of reactive. If we know that this will occur and we EXPECT it to occur, planning ahead and preparing for it could not only save you money, but also save the agony of watching massive drops in your nest egg that you have worked your entire life to save.

---

***Fast Fact:*** *It took the US stock market 18 months to recover from its most recent bear market – the downturn of December 2021.*[60]

---

In my opinion, this is a major value of a good advisor guiding you through retirement, not just caring about the financial aspect of your retirement, but also the emotional toll it can have. Because if you lose 30 percent, in a market drop – say you have $1,000,000 and it drops to $700,000 – and then the market jumps back 30 percent, you are still not even with where you started – 30 percent growth of $700,000 only gets you to $910,000. To bounce back from a 30 percent drop you would need to make a 43 percent return! If you lose 50 percent in a stock market drop, you would need to make a 100 percent return just to get back to even.

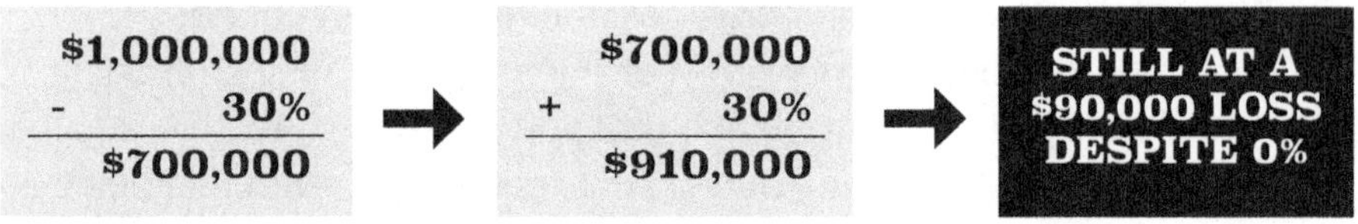


Source: Author's own calculations.

60 Fredlick, Emelia. "What We've Learned From 150 Years of Stock Market Crashes." September 2025, Morningstar, https://www.morningstar.com/economy/what-weve-learned-150-years-stock-market-crashes, Accessed 9/16/2025.

The stock market has historically always gone up in the U.S. over time. Investing in the U.S. stock market means you are investing in U.S. companies which continue to grow over time. I am confident that even if you experience a loss, when properly invested, it will come back over time.

But what do you have less of in retirement? *Time*. Can you really wait for it to come back, or do you need to access your funds to live off of?

Let's say the $1,000,000 that lost 30 percent was also a retirement portfolio that the owner was drawing $50,000 of income off per year to live comfortably. Well now that $1,000,000 dropped to $700,000 with the market drop, the owner takes out $50,000 so he has $650,000, and now that 43 percent return isn't enough. A 43 percent return will only get the account back up to $929,500.

Now let's take this example and play it out over a 25-year retirement using real returns over the past 25 years and a very common portfolio found in employer retirement plans like 401(k) s. In this example, let's assume a $1,000,000 portfolio, with the owner retiring in the year 2000 and planning to withdraw $50,000 annually for 25 years. To account for inflation, we will increase the income by 3 percent each year. We will have the owner of the portfolio invested in the Fidelity Freedom 2030 Fund (ticker FFFEX). Here are the annual returns, income amount, and portfolio value over a 25-year period:

| YEAR | FFFEX PORTFOLIO | INCOME (3% INFLATION) | ACCOUNT VALUE |
|---|---|---|---|
| Retire | | | $1,000,000.00 |
| 2000 | -5.07% | $50,000.00 | $899,300.00 |
| 2001 | -11.69% | $51,500.00 | $742,671.83 |
| 2002 | -17.31% | $53,045.00 | $561,070.34 |
| 2003 | 28.42% | $54,636.35 | $665,890.18 |
| 2004 | 10.45% | $56,275.44 | $679,200.26 |
| 2005 | 8.86% | $57,963.70 | $681,413.70 |
| 2006 | 12.90% | $59,702.61 | $709,613.45 |
| 2007 | 9.27% | $61,493.69 | $713,900.92 |
| 2008 | -36.93% | $63,338.50 | $386,918.81 |
| 2009 | 30.57% | $65,238.66 | $439,961.23 |
| 2010 | 14.04% | $67,195.82 | $434,535.97 |
| 2011 | -3.15% | $69,211.69 | $351,636.39 |
| 2012 | 13.47% | $71,288.04 | $327,713.77 |
| 2013 | 18.13% | $73,426.69 | $313,701.59 |
| 2014 | 5.67% | $75,629.49 | $255,858.98 |
| 2015 | -0.16% | $77,898.37 | $177,551.24 |
| 2016 | 8.13% | $80,235.32 | $111,750.83 |
| 2017 | 19.82% | $82,642.38 | $51,257.46 |
| 2018 | -7.03% | $85,121.65 | -$37,467.59 |
| 2019 | 21.82% | $87,675.30 | -$133,318.32 |
| 2020 | 15.59% | $90,305.56 | -$244,408.21 |
| 2021 | 11.46% | $93,014.73 | -$365,432.12 |
| 2022 | -16.95% | $95,805.17 | -$399,296.54 |
| 2023 | 15.37% | $98,679.33 | -$559,347.75 |
| 2024 | 9.23% | $101,639.71 | -$712,615.25 |

Source: Created using Kwanti Analysis. Past performance is not indicative of future returns.

As you can see in the above chart, the portfolio runs out in only 18 years. The owner of this account will not be able to invest this way and live off the returns for more than 18 years. The portfolio itself averaged 4.96 percent over the same time period, but as you can see, losses hurt more than gains helped.

The owner of this account was also NOT emotionally investing because he was in a managed investment fund that automatically adjusted and rebalanced the investments and risk according to the scheduled date. According to the Employee Benefit Research Institute, these types of "Target-Date Funds" represented 38 percent of the assets in their ICI 401(k) database, and 68 percent of 401(k) participants in the database held target date funds.[61]

These statistics illustrate a very important message: people generally want simplicity in their retirement plan and want to trust a professional resource to help them adjust their plan as they approach retirement. The easiest method for this is inside of the employer plan, however, it might not be the most effective as the retirement age gets closer and hits.

## What Can Be Done Besides an Employer Plan?

Employer provided retirement savings plans are a fantastic place to build and accumulate savings for retirement. Often there is a company match that helps to boost the savings amount quickly and because they are automatically deducted from the paycheck, it functions as a way of "paying yourself first" – meaning that you save for your future before you spend.

The other benefits of the plan include a handful of investment options for the sponsored plan to choose from, some legal protections because the account is held with the company, and higher pre-tax (traditional) and after-tax (ROTH) savings limits.

In fact, for 2025, an employee could save up to $34,750 in either a traditional or ROTH 401(k) depending on their age! And with these savings limits there is no maximum income limit like in traditional IRAs and ROTH IRAs. If you were to save into a ROTH IRA, for example, depending on your age, you would be able to save up to $8,000 per person if you made less than $161,000 as a single person or $240,000 as a married couple filing jointly (Modified Adjusted Gross Income).

As retirement approaches, a person may want a more tailored investment approach—one that aligns with their income plan, incorporates tax conversion strategies, and provides broader investment options than their company plan allows. These, among other reasons, often lead people to move their savings out of the company's plan.

61 Employee Benefit Research Institute. "401(k) Plan Asset Allocation, Account Balances, and Loan Activity in 2022." April 2024, https://www.ebri.org/content/401%28k%29-plan-asset-allocation--account-balances--and-loan-activity-in-2022, Accessed 9/24/2025.

The great news is that they can often do this! Most employer plans allow participants to perform an "in-service" rollover while they are still working at the company if they have reached age 59½ or older. This means that your employer plan, such as your 401(k), stays open and you continue to put your new contributions into it (and the company matches them) for as long as you continue to work there. As for the funds that you have saved up so far, you can "rollover" into an IRA. With the rollover, when done directly to an institution, you will not owe any taxes or have any tax withheld. Once at the new institution and inside of an IRA, the funds can be positioned exactly how you would like them, freeing up any limitations that your company had on investing.

This can be performed with both ROTH and Traditional pre-tax savings. You can also roll over funds when you separate from your employer, and this can be done at any age. In some cases, if your company changes custodians (the investment firm that holds the plan's funds), they may also give you the option to roll over your money. When a modern retiree rolls over their retirement savings into an IRA, there is more flexibility to invest *with purpose* and *on purpose* towards their retirement goals.

## Market Based Investment Options

When investing in the market, there are a lot of options. In fact, there are nearly 6,000 public companies on the U.S. stock exchanges.[62] If that wasn't enough, even though there are only 6,000 stocks, there are 3,243 Exchange-Traded Funds and 8,852 Mutual Funds in the United States. Yes, you read that correctly, there are more funds holding stocks than there are stocks. Here is a simplified overview of each.

62 Dayal, Nikhil. "How Many Stocks Are There?" Benzinga, September 2024, https://www.benzinga.com/money/how-many-stocks-are-there, Accessed 9/24/2025.

**Stocks:**

- Represent ownership in a company.
- Shareholders may earn dividends (company profit payouts) and benefit from capital appreciation (price increase of the stock).
- Prices fluctuate based on company performance, market conditions, and investor sentiment.
- Higher potential returns but come with higher risk.
- Stocks are categorized by small, medium, large, or mega companies, and by value (cheap or on-sale) or growth (expected to grow at a higher rate than its peers).

**Bonds:**

- Represent loans made by investors to entities (e.g., governments, corporations).
- Investors earn interest payments at a fixed rate (coupon) over a set period.
- Considered less risky than stocks, but returns are usually lower.
- Types include government bonds, municipal bonds, and corporate bonds.
- Not all bonds are created equal. Depending on the credit quality (risk of default), callability (the loan getting paid back before due), and term of the loan, the bonds can react to interest rate changes very differently.
- Bonds can be purchased individually or as part of a bond mutual fund or bond ETF.

**Mutual Funds:**

- Pooled investment funds managed by a professional fund manager.
- Diversified portfolios including stocks, bonds, or other assets.
- Investors buy shares in the fund, and the fund's value is calculated at the end of each trading day.

- Often have management fees and are designed for long-term investment goals.

**Exchange-Traded Funds (ETFs):**

- Like mutual funds, but trade on stock exchanges like individual stocks.
- Offer diversification across various assets or sectors.
- Prices fluctuate throughout the trading day.
- Typically have lower expense ratios than mutual funds and no minimum investment requirements.

**Treasuries:**

- Debt securities issued by the U.S. government.
- Are considered one of the safest investments because they are backed by the federal government. Types include:
    - Treasury Bills (T-Bills): Short-term, maturing in less than a year.
    - Treasury Notes (T-Notes): Medium-term, maturing in two-10 years.
    - Treasury Bonds (T-Bonds): Long-term, maturing in 20-30 years.
    - TIPS (Treasury Inflation-Protected Securities): Protect against inflation.
    - Yields are lower due to the low-risk nature of these securities.

**Commodities:**

- Tangible goods that are bought and sold in raw form. Categories include:
    - Energy: Oil, natural gas, coal.
    - Agriculture: Wheat, corn, soybeans, coffee, cotton.
    - Metals: Copper, aluminum, steel (in addition to precious metals).
- Prices are influenced by supply and demand dynamics, geopolitical factors, and weather events. Investors can gain exposure via:

- Future contracts: Agreements to buy/sell at a predetermined price in the future.
- Commodity-focused ETFs.
- Stocks of companies involved in commodity production.
- Commodities are used for diversification and can act as a hedge against inflation or currency fluctuations.

Those are some of the "tools" that can be used to invest in the markets, but they can all fluctuate up and down. They carry risk and should have a specific purpose inside of a portfolio because they also can have specific benefits. Even with bonds, prices typically move in the opposite direction of interest rates—when interest rates rise, bond prices fall, and when interest rates decline, bond prices increase.

However, there are many kinds of bonds, some that can even move in a similar direction as interest rates. With stocks, there are many different types of companies that you can invest in, ranging from small, medium, large, to mega. They can also be classified by sector or industry, by whether they are priced cheaply, and even by geographic location. Once you go down the rabbit hole, you can dissect it in any number of ways.

There are also many ways to analyze a market investment such as fundamentals (based on intrinsic value) or technical (based on how the price has been moving), but none of the analysis is bulletproof. No one has ever been able to correctly and consistently time the market continuously. There are even computer programs that have been developed to trade, called algorithmic trading, that have proven to be inconsistent because they typically trade based on the recent market trend (such as three days of one percent losses). Algorithmic trading can also have significant drawbacks because of the timing and how the market can jump around quickly.

My wife and I were blessed with twin boys to raise. I often feel they teach me about as much as I teach them, they just teach me in a different way. When they were young, we had to learn the hard way why we shouldn't play ball inside the house. We had this big, beautiful window that let in tremendous amounts of light for the house, and it was a solid piece of glass that made it easy to look outside through.

One day though, one of the boys threw a ball and it hit a weak spot in the window, resulting in a massive crack. When we received estimates to replace it, they were shocking. So, after much deliberation, we decided that accidents happen, and they most likely will happen again at some point, as history does tend to repeat itself. So, when we replaced it, we decided that the best choice was to replace it with a window that contained window panes, so that if it did break again, only a portion of the window would be damaged instead of the whole thing. This will protect us in the long run by saving us money. Diversifying an investment portfolio is like putting panes in the window.

When building a retirement portfolio, the most common recommendation is a diversified portfolio. We know from looking at the historical performance of different sectors that the diversified portfolio tends to stay in the middle of the pack. It doesn't shoot up like a rocket ship to the top of the chart in good years, but it also doesn't sink like a stone to the bottom performer in bad years. This way, if one market sector or one type of investment has a damaging year or event, the rest of the portfolio will sustain you, the investor, from catastrophic losses.

Over the long term, the diversified portfolio yields the best results because it rises when the market goes up and loses less when the market drops. And as you get closer to retirement, losses hurt more than gains help.

## Annuities

Annuities are a tool that can be used in retirement planning, but they often seem to be a controversial topic for some people. At the end of the day, it is just another option that may or may not be appropriate, depending on your individual retirement plans. I have met people that have held strong opinions on both sides of the fence—some come in wanting to put all their money into an annuity, while others make it clear that they 'don't believe' in annuities at all. Regardless of beliefs, in my opinion, it just comes down to math.

Given that annuities have been around for so long, and with so many different types, structures, and companies—it's important to dispel common 'myths' about them. After all, 401(k)s have been replacing pensions for decades. But at its core, a pension was essentially an annuity.

Here are 12 common myths that I have heard:

1. ***Myth: Annuities are bad investments.***
    - Reality: Annuities are tools, not inherently good or bad. Their suitability depends on your financial goals, such as securing guaranteed income, protecting against market risk, or managing longevity risk.
2. ***Myth: Annuities are too expensive.***
    - Reality: While some annuities have high fees (e.g., variable annuities with riders), others, like fixed annuities, can have minimal costs. Comparing products and understanding fee structures is key.
3. ***Myth: You lose all your money if you die early.***
    - Reality: Many annuities offer death benefits or guarantees, ensuring your beneficiaries receive the remaining value or income for a specified period.
4. ***Myth: Annuities don't keep up with inflation.***
    - Reality: While some annuities provide fixed payments, others can grow based on market performance or adjust for inflation.
5. ***Myth: Annuities are only for retirees.***
    - Reality: Deferred annuities can be used by individuals in their working years to grow money tax-deferred until retirement. Annuities can also be part of estate or financial planning strategies.
6. ***Myth: Annuities are too complicated.***
    - Reality: Some annuities are straightforward, while others can be more complex. A good financial advisor can help simplify and explain them.

7. ***Myth: You can't access your money in an annuity.***
    - Reality: Most annuities allow partial withdrawals without penalty. Some annuities also offer features like liquidity riders.
8. ***Myth: All annuities are the same.***
    - Reality: Annuities come in many forms, such as fixed, variable, indexed, immediate, and deferred, each with different features, risks, and benefits.
9. ***Myth: Annuities are only for risk-averse individuals.***
    - Reality: Different types of annuities cater to different risk tolerances. Some have no risk of loss while others can still lose money.
10. ***Myth: Insurance companies won't honor annuity payouts.***
    - Reality: Reputable insurance companies are heavily regulated and required to maintain reserves to meet obligations. Choosing highly rated insurers reduces risk.
11. ***Myth: You can get better returns elsewhere.***
    - Reality: Annuities prioritize guaranteed income and security, which may trade off higher returns for lower risk. However, variable or indexed annuities can offer competitive growth potential.
12. ***Myth: Annuities are unnecessary if you have a 401(k) or IRA.***
    - Reality: Annuities can complement these accounts by converting retirement savings into a guaranteed lifetime income stream or providing tax deferral on non-retirement savings.

---

***Fast Fact:*** *Retirees with a guaranteed income reported higher levels of satisfaction and faced fewer affordability challenges.*[63]

---

63 Conway, C. "Research reveals 'clear happiness advantage' for those with annuities." Pensions Age, November 2024, https://www.pensionsage.com/pa/Retirees-with-annuity-enjoy-greater-satisfaction-and-fewer-affordability-struggles.php, Accessed 6/10/2025.

Now not all annuities are the same, which is why it takes experience, education and understanding to figure out if an annuity would be beneficial to your retirement plan and which annuity. Here are the main types split up by how your contribution grows and how it pays:

Based on When Payments Begin:

**Immediate Annuities**

- How it works: Payments start immediately (usually within a month to a year) after a lump sum is paid to the insurance company.
- Purpose: Ideal for people looking for immediate income, often used by retirees.
- Pros: Guaranteed income right away.
- Cons: No access to the principal once payments start.

**Deferred Annuities**

- How it works: Payments begin at a future date (e.g., years after purchase).
- Purpose: Allows for savings and growth during the deferral period before income starts.
- Pros: Accumulation phase allows funds to grow tax-deferred.
- Cons: Longer wait for income (lump sum or monthly).

Based on Growth Method:

**Fixed Annuities**

- How it works: Provides guaranteed interest rates during the accumulation phase and fixed payments during the payout phase.
- Purpose: Ideal for risk-averse investors seeking stable and predictable returns.
- Pros: Low risk, predictable income or growth.
- Cons: Lower potential returns compared to variable or indexed annuities.

**Variable Annuities**

- How it works: Contributions are invested in various subaccounts (like mutual funds). Payments depend on investment performance.
- Purpose: Suitable for individuals willing to take on more risk for potentially higher returns.
- Pros: Potential for higher returns, choice of investment options.
- Cons: Can have high fees, risk of losing principal if investments perform poorly.

**Indexed Annuities**

- How it works: Returns are tied to the performance of a market index (e.g., S&P 500) but include a cap (maximum return) and floor (minimum guarantee).
- Purpose: For those wanting moderate growth potential with less risk than variable annuities.
- Pros: Limited downside risk (or none), potential for growth tied to the market; can have no fees.
- Cons: Caps may limit growth; can have complex fee structures.

<u>Based on Payout Structure:</u>

**Life Annuities**

- How it works: Payments are made for the lifetime of the annuitant, regardless of how long they live.
- Purpose: Protects against outliving retirement savings.
- Pros: Guaranteed lifetime income.
- Cons: No payments to heirs unless a death benefit is included.

**Joint and Survivor Annuities**

- How it works: Provides income for the lifetimes of two individuals (e.g., spouses). Payments continue to the surviving individual.
- Purpose: Ensures income for a surviving spouse.
- Pros: Peace of mind for couples.

Cons: Lower payout amounts compared to

single-life annuities.

**Period Certain Annuities**

- How it works: Guarantees payments for a specific period (e.g., 10 or 20 years). Payments may continue to beneficiaries if the annuitant dies during the period.
- Purpose: Ensures income for a fixed time frame.
- Pros: Guarantees a set number of payments.
- Cons: Payments may stop before the annuitant's death if the period ends.

**Income Rider**

- How it works: Guarantees payments for the life of the annuitant (and sometime the spouse if elected). Some may have inflationary provisions. There can be death benefit protection for beneficiaries in the event of premature passing
- Purpose: Protects and guarantees income for life regardless of how long the life is and leave what's left in the account to beneficiaries.
- Pros: Protects against longevity, consistent guaranteed payments for life, access to principle if needed, death benefit protections.
- Cons: Additional distributions above the income rider guarantees may reduce future payments.

<u>Specialized Annuities:</u>

**Deferred Income Annuities (DIAs)**

- How it works: Purchased now, with payments starting at a future date (e.g., after age 80).
- Purpose: Provides guaranteed income later in life.
- Pros: Higher payments due to deferral.
- Cons: No access to the funds during the deferral period.

**Qualified Longevity Annuity Contracts (QLACs)**

- How it works: A type of deferred income annuity purchased within a retirement account (e.g., 401(k) or IRA), with payments beginning later in life.
- Purpose: Helps manage longevity risk while delaying

Required Minimum Distributions (RMDs).
- Pros: Tax advantages, later-life income.
- Cons: Funds are locked in until payouts begin.

**Variable Indexed Annuities (VIAs)**
- How it works: Combines features of both indexed and variable annuities, offering some protection while providing exposure to market performance.
- Purpose: For those wanting growth potential with partial downside protection.
- Pros: Growth potential with reduced risk.
- Cons: Complex fee structures.

***Real Estate Investing in Retirement***

When you think about retirement, real estate might not be the first thing that comes to mind. However, it can be a powerful way to grow your money and create income during your golden years. Let's explore how real estate investing works, the benefits it offers, and the risks you should consider before diving in.

Real estate investing can come in many forms such as houses, apartments, or commercial buildings. You can make money in two main ways:

1. **Rental Income:** Renting out the property to tenants provides a regular income.
2. **Property Appreciation:** Over time, the value of the property might go up, allowing you to sell it for more than you paid.

<u>Here are some common ways retirees can invest in real estate:</u>

1. **Rental Properties:** Owning houses or apartments that you rent out to tenants.
2. **Real Estate Investment Trusts (REITs):** These are companies that own and manage real estate. You can invest in them like you'd invest in stocks, however, if it is a private REIT, it's typically very challenging to get your money out of the holding and you don't have control over how the company is run or how funds are used.
3. **Vacation Rentals:** Short-term rentals, like Airbnb, can be a

great way to earn income if you own a property in a popular destination. Laws continue to change with these, so check the local area before investing.

4. **Flipping Houses:** Buying homes, fixing them up, and selling them for profit.

Pros of Real Estate Investing in Retirement:

1. **Regular Income:** Rental properties can provide a steady flow of monthly income to cover expenses or enhance your lifestyle.
2. **Appreciation Potential:** Over time, real estate often increases in value, helping you build wealth.
3. **Tax Benefits**: There are tax deductions available for property owners, such as mortgage interest, maintenance costs, and property taxes. Inheritance laws for real estate are also favorable with a step-up in basis.
4. **Diversification:** Real estate can add variety to your investments, reducing the risk of putting all your money in one place.
5. **Tangible Asset:** Unlike stocks or bonds, real estate is something you can see, touch, and use.

Cons of Real Estate Investing in Retirement:

1. **High Upfront Costs:** Buying property requires a lot of money upfront, including a down payment, closing costs, and maintenance.
2. **Ongoing Responsibilities:** Being a landlord can be time-consuming and stressful, especially if you have problem tenants or unexpected repairs.
3. **Market Risks:** Property values can go down during economic downturns, reducing your potential profit.
4. **Illiquidity:** Real estate isn't as easy to sell as stocks or bonds. It might take months to sell a property if you need quick cash.
5. **Management Challenges**: Managing a property can be difficult, especially as you age. Hiring a property manager

can help, but it adds to your expenses. Bad tenants can wipe out profitability very quickly and even cause losses.

Real estate can be a great way to create income and build wealth in retirement, but it's not for everyone. If you enjoy hands-on projects and have the financial resources to invest in, it might be a good fit. However, if you prefer less responsibility or don't want to risk losing money, you might want to stick with other investments. If you have never personally managed real estate and are thinking about doing it in retirement, my suggestion would be to start small and not invest a significant portion of your nest-egg until you have proven results and processes.

If you currently own real estate, it is important to have a plan for retirement. Answering questions before they arise will help bring into focus the other aspects needed in the future to support your real estate. Some of the questions include, how long are you planning on managing the property yourself? At what point do you sell the property? What will you do if it starts to lose money? How will the property transfer after death?

---

***Fast Fact:** Real estate introduces a new asset class that can blend well with traditional investments, buffering against downturns in other market segments, thereby stabilizing your overall financial position.*[64]

---

## Banks and Cash Reserves

During the preparation phase for income and investment planning in retirement, it is important to include in your equation how much cash will be on the side and what to do with it. As with all things, the amount of cash that you like to keep in the

64 UMATechnology. "Pros and Cons of Real Estate Investing After Retirement." UMATechnology, May 2025. https://umatechnology.org/pros-and-cons-of-real-estate-investing-after-retirement/, Accessed 1/16/2026.

bank seems to be largely based on your personal experiences and emotions. I have met individuals with all of their retirement savings in cash because they didn't want the risk of the market, and I have met those that have no cash, and everything invested to "grow" it. I believe there is a happy medium between growth and the stability/flexibility of cash reserves.

First let's answer the question of why we need cash reserves for our retirement plan. They will be the safety valve for emergency expenses like home repairs, helping family members, or medical expenses that we can dip into quickly without disrupting our income plan. They also prevent you from having to sell investments during a market downturn (which we previously discussed) so that you can let your investments recover. The third major reason is that it provides peace of mind to be able to cover day-to-day expenses without penalties or having to wait for a transaction to be processed.

The right amount of cash to hold is somewhere between three-12 months of living expenses. If you have stable income sources like a pension, annuity, or Social Security (or a combination of them) that cover most of your living expenses, then you should need three to six months in cash. If you have most of your income coming from market investments, then having a six-12 month cushion is recommended. Lastly, if you have a major expense like a new car or house purchase in the next one to three years, then holding that amount in cash could be ideal to ensure you don't lose any of the funds due to a market dip at the time you want to purchase the item.

Some of the best places to hold your cash reserves in retirement are a High Yield Savings Account (HYSA), money market funds, certificates of deposit (CDs), or treasury bills/bonds. All these options will earn interest while your cash sits, but there are pros and cons to each. HYSA is fully liquid and FDIC insured; however, the interest rate can fluctuate regularly. Money markets can yield slightly higher amounts but also fluctuate and sometimes have higher minimums and/or fees. CDs will have a more stable interest rate but will be less flexible with access because they might carry penalties for early withdrawals. Treasuries are backed by the government and can have good returns but can be challenging for some to invest and slow to get the funds as needed.

## Investment Strategies

Defining the purpose of your specific investments is the first step to choosing what to invest in. This is why, when it comes to retirement planning, income strategy is prioritized over investment strategy. Another way to put it for any baseball fans – I don't care how fast you can steal a base if you can't manage to ever get on base during a game. So, the first step in determining what your investment strategy should look like, and even how to measure it, is to define your purposes behind the investments. It is important to note that you can have multiple purposes for your investments. If this is the case, then split your investments into different buckets and invest accordingly.

One common purpose is investing for income. When investing for income, we want to minimize the risk of losses for the funds while still growing consistently to keep up with inflation. There are two major indicators to consider when evaluating this style of portfolio – average rate of return and **standard deviation**.

The average rate of return is the average amount of growth that a portfolio has over a given period of time, and the standard deviation is the amount and size of fluctuations (ups and downs) it will experience over a given amount of time. The higher the standard deviation, the riskier the portfolio and the bigger market swings it will experience (both gains and losses). Low risk investors usually want a lower standard deviation portfolio.

In the previous example, we looked at a target-date 2030 portfolio with a 25-year average return of 4.96 percent and a standard deviation of 12.9 percent. If we compare that to an advisor managed portfolio with an average return of 7.38 percent and a standard deviation of six percent over the same time period and take $50,000 out every year (with three percent inflation adjustment) of the $1,000,000 total, we will see a significant difference in results.

| YEAR | FFFEX PORTFOLIO | INCOME (3% INFLATION) | ACCOUNT VALUE | RWD MODERATE | INCOME (3% INFLATION) | ACCOUNT VALUE |
|---|---|---|---|---|---|---|
| Retire | | | $1,000,000.00 | | | $1,000,000.00 |
| 2000 | -5.07% | $50,000.00 | $899,300.00 | 1.97% | $50,000.00 | $969,700.00 |
| 2001 | -11.69% | $51,500.00 | $742,671.83 | -0.24% | $51,500.00 | $915,872.72 |
| 2002 | -17.31% | $53,045.00 | $561,070.34 | -1.97% | $53,045.00 | $844,785.03 |
| 2003 | 28.42% | $54,636.35 | $665,890.18 | 20.07% | $54,636.35 | $959,697.03 |
| 2004 | 10.45% | $56,275.44 | $679,200.26 | 12.28% | $56,275.44 | $1,021,272.39 |
| 2005 | 8.86% | $57,963.70 | $681,413.70 | 7.20% | $57,963.70 | $1,036,840.30 |
| 2006 | 12.90% | $59,702.61 | $709,613.45 | 10.48% | $59,702.61 | $1,085,798.54 |
| 2007 | 9.27% | $61,493.69 | $713,900.92 | 8.35% | $61,493.69 | $1,114,969.03 |
| 2008 | -36.93% | $63,338.50 | $386,918.81 | -12.04% | $63,338.50 | $917,388.25 |
| 2009 | 30.57% | $65,238.66 | $439,961.23 | 17.83% | $65,238.66 | $1,015,719.92 |
| 2010 | 14.04% | $67,195.82 | $434,535.97 | 10.67% | $67,195.82 | $1,056,901.42 |
| 2011 | -3.15% | $69,211.69 | $351,636.39 | 1.78% | $69,211.69 | $1,006,502.57 |
| 2012 | 13.47% | $71,288.04 | $327,713.77 | 10.53% | $71,288.04 | $1,041,199.24 |
| 2013 | 18.13% | $73,426.69 | $313,701.59 | 13.77% | $73,426.69 | $1,111,145.69 |
| 2014 | 5.67% | $75,629.49 | $255,858.98 | 8.17% | $75,629.49 | $1,126,296.81 |
| 2015 | -0.16% | $77,898.37 | $177,551.24 | 1.52% | $77,898.37 | $1,065,518.15 |
| 2016 | 8.13% | $80,235.32 | $111,750.83 | 9.47% | $80,235.32 | $1,086,187.40 |
| 2017 | 19.82% | $82,642.38 | $51,257.46 | 13.64% | $82,642.38 | $1,151,700.98 |
| 2018 | -7.03% | $85,121.65 | -$37,467.59 | -0.97% | $85,121.65 | $1,055,407.83 |
| 2019 | 21.82% | $87,675.30 | -$133,318.32 | 14.79% | $87,675.30 | $1,123,827.34 |
| 2020 | 15.59% | $90,305.56 | -$244,408.21 | 11.56% | $90,305.56 | $1,163,436.22 |
| 2021 | 11.46% | $93,014.73 | -$365,432.12 | 12.54% | $93,014.73 | $1,216,316.39 |
| 2022 | -16.95% | $95,805.17 | -$399,296.54 | -5.87% | $95,805.17 | $1,049,113.45 |
| 2023 | 15.37% | $98,679.33 | -$559,347.75 | 15.45% | $98,679.33 | $1,112,522.15 |
| 2024 | 9.23% | $101,639.71 | -$712,615.25 | 10.87% | $101,639.71 | $1,131,813.61 |

Source: Created using Kwanti Analysis. Past performance does not indicate future performance.

As you can see in the above chart, we added the three columns onto the same chart we had earlier in this chapter. With the target-date fund, the income runs out after 18 years and there is no money left in the account. Getting a slightly higher return with a lower standard deviation (lower risk) shows that after 15 years of income increasing with inflation, we are left with about the same amount ($1,131,813.61) that we started with in the account. This shows the power of investing *with* purpose, especially when the purpose is income.

To achieve the result of lowering the risk (standard deviation) while still getting a reasonable return, we need to build a portfolio that can grow as the economy rises, but is partially shielded and defensive when the economy drops. This type of portfolio is going to contain a wide range of investments, typically with safer strategies and defensive positions, balanced with growth opportunities and high performing stocks. It may involve an individualized mix of the following:

- **Active Investing:** Buying and selling positions based on the market outlook.
- **Passive Investing:** Minimizing buying and selling to mirror an index performance.
- **Growth Investing:** Investing in high growth-oriented companies.

- **Value Investing:** Buying investments that are undervalued based on fundamentals.
- **Bond/CD/Annuity Ladders:** Buying different maturity dates at sequential intervals.
- **Indexed Annuities:** Participating when the market is up, but not losing when the market drops.
- **Alternative Investments:** Investments that don't typically correlate with the rest of the market movement.

Depending on your investment goals, you might have an income "bucket" of lower-risk investments from which to draw income, paired with a higher-risk 'bucket' that you don't touch for 10+ years. This allows you to ride the market's highs and lows while knowing that any income you need will come from the income "bucket".

Strategically investing for tax planning also layers onto how much risk you will be taking with your investments. We will cover taxes in subsequent chapters, however from an investment strategy perspective, it is significant. If you have or will be having ROTH funds in your retirement planning, typically those funds are intended to be the last investments used as income. That is because ROTH funds grow tax-free and are not subject to required minimum distributions, so you never have to take them out unless you want to. ROTH accounts are typically going to be invested in higher risk, growth-oriented investments, so that we can maximize the tax-free growth. In a portfolio that has a mixture of ROTH and Traditional IRA funds, the Traditional IRA will be subject to the required minimum distributions, forcing you to take the money out of the Traditional IRA.

As you get closer to the date of the Required Minimum Distribution, you might separate the portion that will be distributed and put it in lower risk investments in case the market drops. Furthermore, if you have a taxable account like a brokerage account that you will owe capital gains on each year, you might consider investing those holdings into individual stocks or passive ETF funds for the tax advantages, otherwise you will experience what is known as "tax drag". "Tax drag" is when dividends, capital gains, and interest eat away at the investment returns on the account. For example, if you experience a 10 percent return, but two percent of that is taken away by taxes from buying and selling, then the real return is only eight percent. This can happen inside mutual funds as part of their normal portfolio turnover.

There are thousands of investment options in the market, so before you start trying to figure out the "best" investment, I would first consider the strategic purpose that you will want from the investment. It can serve more than one purpose, but define the purpose(s), then pick the investment that most closely aligns with the goals.

Warren Buffett once said, "Why risk what you have for what you don't need." If your retirement income analysis shows that you will not run out of money, then why take unnecessary risks which could cause running out of money to happen?

Instead, set the money aside that will hit your income goals and invest it appropriately in the income bucket, then take the leftovers (which could be significant) and take as much or as little risk as you want to. You could swing for the fence (high risk) with the leftovers knowing that if the market drops and you lose 50 percent in a down year, you will still be OK because your income bucket is secure and will provide for you, forever.

## Conclusion

When the market isn't doing well, that's when people tend to panic and reach out for help. They suddenly realize how important it is to take care of the money they've worked so hard to save for retirement. Don't wait until you lose the money before assessing your financial phase and getting some kind of retirement plan in place.

## CHAPTER FIVE CHALLENGE:

On a scale of 1-10, how much risk do you want to take in your portfolio (with 1 being the lowest, and 10 being the highest)?

0 1 2 3 4 5 6 7 8 9 10

At this stage of your life, what is the maximum loss that you feel like you can sustain?

-10% -20% -30% -40% -50% -60%

Do you prefer to manage investments yourself, or to pay someone else to manage them? How about in 10 years?

________________________________________

________________________________________

________________________________________

Do you have retirement funds in employer plans that could be rolled into an IRA and consolidated?

________________________________________

________________________________________

________________________________________

When was the last time that you had your portfolio professionally analyzed?

________________________________________

________________________________________

________________________________________

What types of investments are included/excluded from your portfolio? Why? And should that change as you change life stages?

________________________________________

________________________________________

________________________________________

Have you considered adding annuities or real estate to your portfolio? Why or why not?

______________________________________________

______________________________________________

______________________________________________

How much cash is the right amount for you?

______________________________________________

______________________________________________

______________________________________________

Do your investments align with your purpose for your money?

______________________________________________

______________________________________________

______________________________________________

If your portfolio is over $250,000 and you would like a complimentary portfolio review and analysis, reach out to us in one of three ways:

- By phone: (636) 388-7722
- By email: Info@RetirementWealthDesign.com
- Visit our website at: RetirementWealthDesign.com

# CHAPTER SIX

## STRATEGIC TAX PLANNING

*"In this world, nothing is certain except death and taxes."*
*– Benjamin Franklin*

Do you think that Benjamin Franklin was focused on his retirement when he said the above quote? Probably not. Men didn't live that long back in Franklin's days so, outliving your money wasn't the problem that it is today.

In retirement, it's not about how much you make, it's about how much you keep after taxes. After all, that is what you will be spending. The challenge becomes, for most retirees, that it can feel like it's too late to do anything about it. You have been saving for your entire career into mostly pre-tax accounts, so now all your savings are stacked in those accounts. If you go to most CPAs, they are focused on saving you money this year on your taxes, so recommending you take money out now and pay the taxes goes against what value they might feel they bring (even if it will save you taxes in the long run). Does it even matter? Won't taxes go down while you are in retirement because income will go down?

Remember – it's about what you keep – as in, take home pay. Most retirees that I work with want to keep their standard of living the same as when they were working, if not a little bit better. In fact, I have been told, "If I can't keep my same lifestyle, I might as well just keep working!" So, if your lifestyle stays the same, then the income will need to be similar after-tax, and to get a similar after-tax income, you will need a similar pre-tax income.

The caveat here will be that if you have major expenses that suddenly vanish in retirement, such as debt or your mortgage, then you potentially will not need as much income. However, in some cases, as a mortgage gets paid off in retirement, that income need could be replaced with healthcare expenses.

So, will tax rates go down, stay the same, or go up while you are retired? I don't have a crystal ball, so to answer this question we need to look at the history of taxation and make an informed decision. After all, if taxes go down when you are retired, then keep as much money in pre-tax sheltered accounts now because you will keep more later.

If taxes go up when you are retired though, you might want to move taxes into after-tax accounts to keep more of your money. And if taxes stay the same, it won't matter if you pay taxes now or later if you are in a similar bracket.

Let's look at the history of taxes to help us form an opinion of where taxes may be headed.

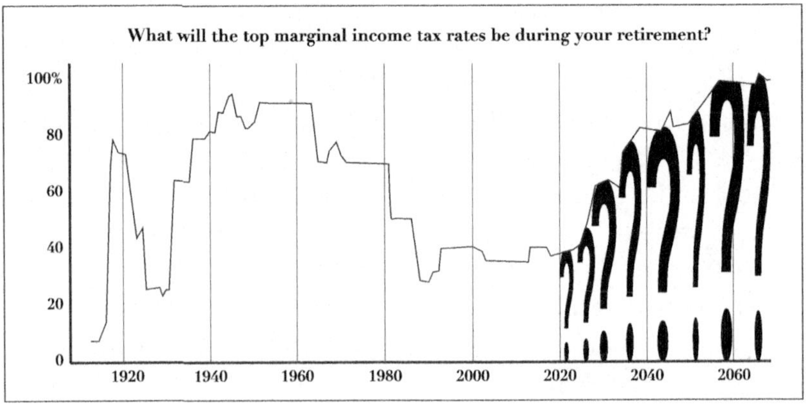


Source: Magellan Financial using data from the Urban-Brookings Tax Policy Center, "Historical Individual Income Tax Parameters: 1913 to 2018"

If we begin around 1940, you can see the U.S. national debt skyrockets as we paid for World War II. Equipment was being built to fight the war, and our boys were overseas keeping us safe at home. The top U.S. tax brackets also rose which brought more revenue to the U.S. government, which it could then use to pay down the national debt. After the war, the debt began coming down and the tax brackets followed. If you look at the chart towards the middle, find the year 1978. The U.S. national debt had been coming down and the tax brackets had been falling.

The stock market at that time had also been averaging double digit growth. November 6th, 1978, is when the 401(k) passed through Congress as part of the IRS code. The message behind them to the public was clear – save into your 401(k) to save on taxes now, let that money grow tax-deferred because you will pay less taxes in retirement and have more money. Looking at this chart, I would tend to agree with that message to the public. The challenge is that after that time period, when we look at the U.S. national debt, it started to creep back up. Then it continues to run up, surpassing the GDP of the country. As of the second quarter of 2025, the U.S. national debt was $36.2 trillion, which represented 119.4 percent of the nation's GDP of $30.3 trillion.

Simply put, we are producing $29 trillion of value as a country per year but are in $36 trillion worth of debt. Nine percent of the federal spending goes towards just maintaining the national debt! Yet, if we look at the tax rates, we are still historically low compared to where they were in the 1900s. Right now, I don't believe it feels like taxes are low for most Americans, however, the chart above demonstrates otherwise. There are many changes that can be made to effect this, but I pose the question again, do you think taxes are going down, staying the same, or going up?

## Tax Treatment of Accounts

Some might call taxes the biggest retirement risk to the modern retiree. Let's say, for example, that you want to live off of $8,000 per month, so you might need to take $10,000 out of your account, withhold the taxes, and take home the $8,000 per month. Now let's say that taxes go up. You will have to make a choice: either learn to live off of less income per month and keep the same withdrawal amount of $10,000 or take more money out of your accounts to stay at $8,000 per month and run the risk of running out money (because you are now taking out more each month). It isn't a good choice to have to make, is it?

In order to plan ahead, we first need to assess the situation. Where is your money held? Taxable, tax-deferred, and tax-free accounts are categories of investment accounts, each with unique tax implications. Here's how they differ:

**1. Taxable Accounts**

These accounts have no special tax advantages, meaning income and gains are taxed in the year they are earned.

- Examples: Brokerage accounts, savings accounts, checking accounts.
- Tax Treatment:
    - Interest Income: Taxed as ordinary income in the year it's earned.
    - Dividends: Qualified dividends are taxed at the lower long-term capital gains rate, while non-qualified dividends are taxed as ordinary income.
    - Capital Gains: Realized gains (when you sell an asset) are taxed. Short-term gains (held <1 year) are taxed as ordinary income, while long-term gains (held >1 year) are taxed at favorable rates.
    - Losses: Capital losses can offset gains and up to $3,000 of ordinary income per year.
- Benefit: Flexibility in contributions and withdrawals without restrictions.

**2. Tax-Deferred Accounts**

These accounts allow investments to grow without immediate taxation, but taxes are owed upon withdrawal.

- Examples: Traditional IRA, 401(k), 403(b), TSP, annuities.
- Tax Treatment:
    - Contributions: Often tax-deductible (e.g., pre-tax 401(k) contributions), reducing taxable income for the year.
    - Growth: Investments grow tax-free until withdrawn.
    - Withdrawals: Taxed as ordinary income. Early withdrawals (before age 59½) may incur a 10 percent penalty unless an exception applies.

- Benefit: Defers taxes, potentially lowering tax bills during high-earning years and spreading them out in retirement when income might be lower.

**3. Tax-Free Accounts**

These accounts allow investments to grow and be withdrawn tax-free, provided certain conditions are met.

- Examples: Roth IRA, Roth 401(k), Health Savings Accounts (HSAs) for qualified medical expenses, some cash-value life insurance.
- Tax Treatment:
    - Contributions: Made with after-tax dollars (no immediate tax deduction).
    - Growth: Investments grow tax-free.
    - Withdrawals: Tax-free if qualified (e.g., after age 59½ and meeting the 5-year rule for Roth IRAs or a policy loan from cash-value life insurance).
    - HSAs: Contributions are tax-deductible, growth is tax-free, and withdrawals for qualified expenses are tax-free.
    - Life Insurance: Death benefit is generally tax-free if the premiums were paid with after-tax funds.
- Benefit: No taxes on withdrawals, which is particularly advantageous in retirement.

## COMPARISON AT A GLANCE

| FEATURE | TAXABLE | TAX-DEFERRED | TAX-FREE |
|---|---|---|---|
| CONTRIBUTIONS | After-Tax | Pre-tax (typically) | After-Tax |
| GROWTH TAXATION | Taxed annually | Tax-deferred | Tax-free |
| WITHDRAWAL TAXATION | Gains taxed | Fully taxed as income | Usually tax-free |
| WITHDRAWAL RULES | No restrictions | Age or purpose limits | Age or purpose limits |

Source: Author's own calculations.

## Strategy for Using These Accounts

- Tax Diversification: Use a mix of these accounts to manage tax liability in retirement.
- Tax-Loss Harvesting: Selling investments at a loss to offset capital gains or up to $3,000 of ordinary income, reducing their overall tax liability, while often reinvesting in similar assets to maintain portfolio balance in a taxable account.
- Tax Bracket Management: Withdraw strategically from tax-deferred and taxable accounts to minimize taxes.
- Roth Conversions: Consider converting tax-deferred accounts to Roth accounts during low-income years to lock in tax-free growth.

By understanding how these accounts work, you can optimize your savings and minimize taxes throughout your life and retirement. In many cases, withdrawing money in order – 1. Taxable, 2. Tax-deferred, 3. Tax-free – can make the most sense for retirees. This is because you are letting your tax-free assets grow longer (which should mean larger) and will be tax-free income. The same goes for the tax-deferred assets, letting them grow larger, unincumbered by "tax-drag" as discussed earlier.

## ROTH Conversions

So, what happens when all or some of your retirement savings are already in pre-tax, traditional accounts? Can you convert them to a ROTH account! Yes, you can take money from a pre-tax account and move it into a ROTH account without penalties, you just must pay the income taxes on what you convert.

There are many reasons why you *would* or *would NOT* want to perform ROTH conversions, which we will cover. But at the highest level, it's kind of like taking your car from the U.S. to the U.K.; it is still going to be the same car that you are driving, there are just going to be different rules for the road. Converting savings from pre-tax to ROTH still allow you to invest the same way, there will just be different rules for how and when you can take money out.

Let's start with how it works. Let's say that you want to convert $100,000 from your Traditional IRA to your ROTH IRA. There are no income limits to do so and there is no limit on how much you can convert in a single year. When you transfer the money, you will owe both federal and state (if applicable) income taxes on the conversion, but if you are over 59½, you can withhold the taxes on the conversion without penalty, otherwise you will need to pay them out of pocket. So, if you convert $100,000 and are in the 24 percent federal tax bracket, you will owe $24,000 federal taxes on the conversion. And if your state income tax is 5 percent, you will owe $5,000 in state income taxes.

However, now that the savings is in a ROTH account, it will grow tax-free for the rest of your life. There are also no required minimum distributions, so the money can stay in there as long as you'd like. At whatever time you choose to take it out, you will not owe any taxes, and if you pass away, it will inherit tax-free. This is why when it comes to taking money out, ROTH is typically the last bucket to pull from.

However, on the converted funds there is a 5-year rule in place, meaning that any funds that you convert, you should not plan on touching for at least 5 years, otherwise there could be a penalty on what you take out.

ROTH Conversions are *NOT* ideal for some modern retirees. It largely depends on your goals in retirement and your current/ future tax brackets.

To discuss this further, let's first review how the tax brackets work at the federal level. I think of them like filling up a glass of water. As the water goes into the glass, the first amount fills the bottom of the glass. This would be the 10 percent tax bracket and your first $11,925 of income if you are single ($23,850 for married filing jointly). As the water continues to fill the glass, so does the next tax bracket. Any income between $11,925 - $48,475 for a single person is taxed at 12 percent ($23,850-$96950 MFJ).

The next level will be any income between $48,475-$103,350, which is taxed at 22 percent ($96,950-$206,700 MFJ). These tax brackets are for 2025 and continue for the 24, 32, 35, and 37 percent brackets, so check in your current year what the tax brackets are for more information.

The purpose of this explanation is that it can be confusing sometimes, but any money that you convert to a ROTH will not affect your other income, it will only affect the amount of taxes that you will pay on the ROTH funds. So, when considering ROTH conversions, you may want to calculate how much you can convert and stay in the current tax bracket while also including the standard deduction. Because ROTH conversions *do* count as income, you will also want to measure the "ripple effects" that they can have on the other areas tied to your income levels.

If you are receiving subsidies for the Affordable Care Act exchange, this can cause you to lose your subsidy. Your income will be reported to CMS, so it can impact how much you will pay for Medicare in two years (IRMAA). If you pay capital gains taxes on a brokerage account, it could bump up the capital gains bracket that you are in. Measuring all of the impacts will be important to help you make informed financial decisions.

A ROTH conversion often doesn't make sense if you are in a significantly higher tax bracket now, compared to where you will be in the future. For example, if you are in the 32 percent bracket now because you are working a high-income job, but you will be in the 12 percent tax bracket when you retire in five years, then paying 32 percent taxes on a ROTH conversion now is going to most likely result in overpaying in taxes instead of saving in taxes.

A ROTH conversion might not make sense if you are currently collecting Social Security and your required minimum distribution is less than the standard deduction. In this "tax-free retirement zone," you're likely not paying any taxes on your Social Security income.

A ROTH conversion can make a lot of sense in many cases though where someone has saved $500,000 or more in a pre-tax account.

For example, let's take a single individual, age 60, who makes $80,000 per year, and will retire in five years. This person has

$700,000 saved in a 401(k) and is planning on living off of $60,000 per year in retirement, including Social Security. This person is also concerned that taxes will rise significantly in the future.

Looking at the situation, it could make sense to begin a conversion strategy, converting $35,000 per year for the next five years. In doing so, this person might owe $7,700 in federal taxes (and state if applicable) per $35,000 conversion, so if they withheld the taxes, they would have $136,500 in a ROTH IRA that could now grow tax-free and be taken out tax-free. This would need to be looked at each year and invested appropriately for the strategy to make sense.

The total tax savings from just these five years of conversions could be $33,904 while alive, and $116,900 extra inheritance if the money only grows at a 5.71 percent average![65]

The larger the investment accounts, the larger the potential tax savings. When performing ROTH conversions, it is important to do the math and weigh all of the ripple effects before making the conversion because once done, it cannot be undone. This is why we evaluate every year and make the decisions each year at a time.

---

***Fast Fact:*** *An estimated $15.75 billion in federal revenues will be generated from 2020 through 2029 due to the changes passed by the Secure Act affecting non-spousal IRAs.*[66]

---

## Required Minimum Distributions (RMDs)

Even if you don't want to, you will be forced to take out money from your pre-tax accounts at a certain age. It was 70½ years old, then 72, and is now 73. In the year 2033, it will be 75 years old (for those born in 1960 or later). Yes, the rules keep

65 Data on File. Money Guide Pro software used to calculate tax savings.
66 Kurt, Daniel, What Is the SECURE Act and How Could It Affect Your Retirement? Investopedia, April 2024, https://www.investopedia.com/what-is-secure-act-how-affect-retirement-4692743 Accessed 9/20/2025.

changing, so it's important to stay up to date on them.

I often get asked, "Why do I have to take the money out?" Well, I think that it is because the IRS wants their tax revenue from these accounts and the only way to get it is if you take the money out. It is important to note that if you reach RMD age but are still working, you may not have to take an RMD out of your active 401(k) for as long as you work.

Strategy in your RMD planning can be critical depending on your specific situation. For the purposes of this section, I am going to discuss three common strategies that can be used when addressing RMDs.

1. **Combining RMDs to Distribute from one IRA:** Sometimes people have more than one IRA in their name. You can invest one of the IRAs with the intention of taking the initial RMDs from that amount. What you will need to do is calculate the total RMD needed from all your IRAs, then distribute it from one. The key to this strategy is the IRAs have to be in the exact same name. You cannot mix inherited IRAs with traditional IRAs or spousal IRAs. Consult a professional before attempting this strategy.
2. **Qualified Charitable Distributions (QCDs):** If you give charitably or want to give charitably in retirement, as long as it is a legally acceptable charity, you can give to the charity directly from your IRA. What this does is it completely cuts taxation and the IRS out of these funds. You did not pay taxes on the funds going into the pre-tax account and if the check is written from the IRA directly to the charity, no taxes will be owed on the money coming out of the account. However, this QCD will still qualify as your Required Minimum Distribution!
3. **Paying for a ROTH Conversion using the RMD:** If you do not want or need your RMD, you are not able to directly convert the RMD to a ROTH IRA; it is against the tax law. But you can use the RMD to pay the taxes on a ROTH conversion. To do this, first, you'll need to figure

out the RMD amount for the year, let's say for example it is $25,000, then subtract the taxes you will owe from that RMD netting you $20,000 of income. You can then calculate the amount you are able to convert from your traditional IRA to a ROTH IRA that will cost $20,000 in taxes. Hypothetically it might cost $20,000 in taxes to convert $74,400 from a traditional IRA to a ROTH IRA. So, you would make a separate ROTH conversion transaction of $74,400, then pay the $20,000 out of pocket that you received from your RMD. This benefits you because you just moved $74,400 into the tax-free category to grow AND you lowered your RMD for the following year since you'll have $74,400 less in your traditional IRA.

Let's walk through an example of the benefits of tax planning for your retirement. Let's say, for example, John and Joan Smith saved $2,000,000 for retirement in pre-tax accounts and are retiring now at 66 years old. Their Social Security payments will be $60,000 per year and they want to take an additional $50,000 pre-tax from their investments each year to live off of and leave the rest to their kids.

Let's assume that they are paying 22 percent taxes and a six percent average return on their investments. If we split their money into an income fund and an inheritance fund, we can provide the $50,000 income per year using $1,000,000 until age 95 when they pass away. But what should we do with the other $1,000,000?

- **Option A:** We follow the traditional format and let it grow six percent per year in the IRA until they are forced to take it out age 73. When they take it out at age 73, we pay the taxes on the money and reinvest it into a taxable account to let it grow for inheritance.
    - Pay $431,478 in taxes on the RMDs
    - Pay $313,224 in taxes on the growth of the RMDs

  - that were reinvested
  - Beneficiaries pay $224,957 in income taxes on the account value left in the IRA at the time of death
  - Total taxes: $969,659
- **Option B:** We convert to ROTH IRA to the top of the 24 percent until all of the $1,000,000 is converted. Then we let it grow tax-free without touching it and it is inherited tax-free.
  - Pay $415,706.20 in taxes on the ROTH conversions
  - Total taxes: $415,659

By utilizing Option B and performing ROTH conversions to plan ahead, John and Joan are able to save $554,000 in taxes!

## Missed Opportunity Often Overlooked

The tax code regularly changes and often evolves from president to president and Congress to Congress. As part of the constant evolution, it often increases in complexity which can cause subtle opportunities to go unnoticed. One of those opportunities has recently occurred with the passing of the One Big Beautiful Bill Act (OBBBA).

The recent opportunity in the current tax code is that the standard deduction for a person over the age of 65 years old has escalated to $23,750 per year starting in 2025. This is due to a $15,750 base, $2,000 age-based deduction, and a $6,000 senior bonus deduction (with phase out limits).

The standard deduction of $23,750 per year allows for those between the ages of 65 and their Required Minimum Distribution (RMD) age to use that full deduction potential by utilizing ROTH Conversions. If your taxes for the year fall under the standard deduction, you now have the ability to convert funds from traditional IRA to ROTH IRA and potentially not have to pay taxes on the conversion as long as the taxes owed fall under that deduction amount.

When you convert money from traditional IRA to ROTH IRA, that converted amount is taxed as ordinary income in the year of the conversion. But if your total taxable income (after deductions) is below your standard deduction, some or all of that ROTH conversion can be done tax-free. Even if you convert more than the standard deduction amount, the excess simply falls into the 10 percent or 12 percent tax brackets.

Capitalizing on this opportunity essentially allows you to use your standard deduction as a tax-free ROTH conversion bucket instead of letting the deduction go unused.

## Importance of Cost-Basis Adjustments

The "cost-basis" is the price that you paid for an investment, plus any costs of fees or improvements. This is vital to understand when it comes to taxable accounts because when you sell the investment in that account, you are going to get taxed on the PROFIT minus the COST BASIS.

This means that if you sold a stock for $150 that you had bought for $100, you will owe taxes on the $50 of profit that you made. Now for similar investment classes, you are able to cancel out your losses against your profits. You can potentially even deduct up to $3,000 of losses against you working income in a year.

*Why does this matter?* First, it matters because if your investments are not managed in a way that is efficiently monitoring and selling/buying according to how much taxes you will owe, then you are essentially paying for your taxes with your profits. Second, there are special rules, such as 1035 exchanges and 1031 exchanges, where you can trade similar investments without triggering the tax payments. Instead, when you use these exchanges, the cost-basis just carries over. Now, there are many particulars when it comes to these, so additional understanding is needed before performing. Thirdly, it matters because when planning for your legacy, cost-basis adjustments are important for the beneficiaries of your estate.

Stock holdings and real estate will get step-up in basis upon your death, meaning that your beneficiaries won't have to pay taxes on the profit that you gained during your lifetime. For example, let's say you purchased a vacation home for $300,000 in 2012. If you passed away in 2025, and the property was valued at $750,000, your beneficiaries would not have had to pay the taxes on the appreciation. Instead, the cost-basis would be adjusted to the value that it is at the time of death, so their cost basis would be $750,000. If they choose to sell it for $750,000 at that time, they will owe no taxes. If they hold it and sell it 10 years later for $1,000,000, they will owe taxes on $250,000 of profit ($1,000,000 - $750,000 = $250,000). This is a major benefit of leaving taxable assets as inheritance.

## Estate Taxes

After a person passes away, their estate could be subject to estate taxes, which can cause a major reduction in the amount that the beneficiaries would receive.

With the passing of the One Big Beautiful Bill Act (OBBBA) in July 2025, the federal estate tax exemption for 2026 was permanently increased to $15 million per individual. This contrasts with the previous law, which would have automatically cut the exemption to an estimated $7 million at the end of 2025. A person would need an estate larger than the exemption at the time of death for the estate to be further taxed.

When the estate is taxed, those taxes are determined by adding up all of the assets in the estate, subtracting the deductions for this like debts, charitable donations, and property to the surviving spouse, and then applying the exemption. Anything over the exemption will be taxed at the 40 percent estate tax rate.

Beneficiaries may then be "double taxed" if part of their inheritance is in an IRA or 401(k) because the estate has to pay the 40 percent taxes on the account, and then the beneficiaries have to pay income taxes on the inheritance. In the past, the exemption has been far less than $15 million. So as your estate grows in value, consider planning methods that would be beneficial in case there is a legislative change to this amount prior to your death.

Planning for large estates is critical to begin early on as it takes time to position assets for the legacy plan. Common tools to use are gifting, irrevocable life insurance trusts, charitable remainder trusts, and family foundations, among others.

- **Gifting:** You are allowed to gift $19,000 per recipient, per year. These funds are removed from your estate, and because the exclusion limit is $19,000, you don't have to file a gift tax return and can potentially avoid paying gift tax.
- **Irrevocable Life Insurance Trust (ILIT):** This is a special trust that holds and manages a life insurance policy. It helps to reduce estate taxes, protect assets, and controls the distribution of the funds. You can either get a new policy or transfer a current policy into the name of the trust, but you must survive for three years after the transfer for the policy to be excluded from your estate. You can make gifts to the trust for the premiums ($19,000/year) so they fall within the annual gift exclusion limit.
- **Charitable Remainder Trust (CRT):** This allows you to donate to charity while providing income for yourself or your beneficiaries. You create a trust and move your funds, like an IRA, property, or stocks, into the trust. The account continues to grow and you are allowed a certain amount of income from it. Upon death, what is left in the trust goes to the charity that you designated. You also may qualify for a significant tax deduction when you set up the trust equal to the estimated amount that will go to the charity. Often individuals combine this strategy with an ILIT so that they get the tax break from the CRT while also leaving inheritance for loved ones and funding the ILIT from the payments of the CRT.
- **Family Foundations:** A private charitable foundation established and funded by a family. It allows members of the family to work together to make grants to non-profit organizations and causes they care about, while also creating tax benefits and income for the family. The family often controls the foundation and as such, is able to get paid administrative wages. The foundation is a tax-exempt organization so any contributions are tax-deductible and grow tax-free, as long as they distribute a minimum (typically five percent annually) for charitable purposes and follow regulatory laws.

## Conclusion

It was the judge, Learned Hand, who once said, "There are two systems of taxation in our country: one for the informed and one for the uninformed." Nowhere is this more evident than during retirement.

The goal when doing a Roth conversion is to pay the taxes owed on this money while you are in the lowest possible income tax bracket so that you and your family can enjoy tax-free withdrawals later. Be strategic. By doing your tax planning now, you can set things up so that more of this money is yours to keep.

## CHAPTER SIX CHALLENGE:

Do you have a Strategic Tax Plan for retirement?

________________________________________

________________________________________

________________________________________

Do you believe that taxes will go up, go down, or stay the same over the next 10-20 years?

________________________________________

________________________________________

________________________________________

What percentage of your savings is in Taxable ______, Tax-Deferred ______, and Tax-Free ______ type accounts?

________________________________________

________________________________________

________________________________________

Have you considered ROTH conversions? How much will it cost versus how much will it save?

________________________________________

________________________________________

________________________________________

What is your plan for your Required Minimum Distributions (RMDs)?

_______________________________________________

_______________________________________________

_______________________________________________

Will you be tithing or donating to charity during your retirement? What strategies will you use in order to save on taxes?

_______________________________________________

_______________________________________________

_______________________________________________

Visit **www.retirementwealthdesign.com** to use our free TAX TOOL calculator and see if Strategic Tax Planning would benefit you.

# CHAPTER SEVEN

## HEALTHCARE IN RETIREMENT

*"Finance is not merely about making money.*
*It's about achieving our deep goals and*
*protecting the fruits of our labor."*
*~ Robert J. Shiller, economist*

Healthcare costs continue to rise in the United States and continue to be a major focus of retirement planning. For example, according to the most recent EBRI Retirement Confidence Survey, 38 percent of retirees find their health care and dental expenses to be higher than expected, plus those that have yet to retire report that the cost of healthcare hinders their ability to save.[67]

The majority of clients that I meet with who are worried about long-term care costs typically had a parent that needed long-term care. These clients saw their parents' bills firsthand, so they know how high these expenses can get. Clients with children often share that they don't want to become a burden on them in later years due to potential healthcare needs, while those without children frequently express uncertainty about who would care for them

In my family, we have had grandparents that needed care, suffered from dementia, cancer, and other ailments, and needed to relocate to facilities to receive qualified care. If you have gone through that with loved ones, you know it is not easy and each situation is never the same. The purpose of this chapter is to shine a light on considerations as you put your retirement plan in place.

67 Retirement Confidence Survey, 2025, EBRI, https://www.ebri.org/content/full/2025-ebri-greenwald-retirement-confidence-survey Accessed 8/11/2025.

## Early Retirement

Thirty percent of non-retired consumers ages 61 to 65, known as Peak 65 consumers, are contemplating postponing retirement, while financial advisors say 28 percent of their clients have already delayed retirement.[68] And one of the major concerns topping the list in retirement is health issues. The greatest worries include experiencing a major physical health event (67 percent), becoming physically dependent on others (65 percent), and facing cognitive decline (57 percent).[69] And while this can be a valid concern, I am of the opinion that a person should not delay early retirement just because of health concerns. Instead, if planned for properly, the cost of healthcare can be built into your income plan, and you can retire comfortably knowing that you can afford your healthcare before Medicare age. We even have some people utilize different strategies if they are looking for an option other than just paying out of pocket for it, such as:

- Work a lower-stress, lower paying job that provides healthcare until 65.
- Work part-time to make just enough to pay for a personal healthcare plan.
- Work at an employer that provides healthcare but only requires 30 hours of work per week.

There are many perspectives when it comes to healthcare, but the bottom line is this: what does your plan allow for, and what can your income support? Many people that I have met with think that early retirement is out of reach but when we put together the income plan, they can easily afford the healthcare and not risk running out of money or disrupting their other retirement goals. When shopping for healthcare plans in early retirement, there are now many options available:

68 Alliance for Lifetime Income. 2025 Protected Retirement Income & Planning Study, August 2025. https://www.protectedincome.org/wp-content/uploads/2025/08/2025-PRIP-Study-Chapter-1-FINAL-070925.pdf, Accessed 9/23/2025

69 Ibid.

1. **COBRA Coverage**
   - What it is: Allows you to continue your employer-sponsored health insurance for up to 18-36 months after leaving your job.
   - Pros: Same coverage as when employed.
   - Cons: Expensive, as you pay the full premium plus a two percent administrative fee.
2. **Health Insurance Marketplace (Affordable Care Act)**
   - What it is: You can purchase health insurance through the federal or state marketplace at HealthCare.gov or your state exchange.
   - Pros: Tax credits and subsidies may lower costs based on your income.
   - Cons: Coverage and costs vary; plans may include high deductibles.
3. **Retiree Health Insurance**
   - What it is: Some employers offer health insurance for retired employees until they qualify for Medicare.
   - Pros: Seamless transition from your workplace plan.
   - Cons: Not all employers offer this, and coverage may be limited.
4. **Health Sharing Ministries**
   - What it is: Non-profit organizations where members share healthcare costs.
   - Pros: Often lower cost than traditional insurance.
   - Cons: Limited coverage; not a guarantee of payment.
5. **Spouse's Health Insurance**
   - What it is: If your spouse is employed and has coverage, you may be able to join their plan.
   - Pros: Familiar provider network and potentially lower costs.
   - Cons: Adds cost to your spouse's premiums.
6. **Medicaid**
   - What it is: State and federally funded program providing free or low-cost coverage to low-income individuals.
   - Pros: Affordable or free.
   - Cons: Eligibility is income-dependent, and coverage varies

by state.

**7. Private Health Insurance**

- What it is: Purchase directly from an insurer outside of the ACA marketplace.
- Pros: Broad plan choices.
- Cons: Often more expensive without subsidies.

## Medicare

For a couple that turns the age of 65 and retires, the average cost for Medicare in their lifetime will be $330,000 throughout retirement.[70] This includes premiums, co-pays, deductibles, covered prescriptions and non-covered prescriptions. That statistic, when I first read it, changed my view point on the common phrase "health is wealth" because after reading that cost, maybe the phrase should be "health costs wealth". There are many rules to Medicare, planning and options, but here is an overview with some important timeframes:

*Parts of Medicare*

**1. Medicare Part A (Hospital Insurance)**

- Covers inpatient hospital stays, skilled nursing facility care, hospice, and some home health services.
- Cost: Usually free if you or your spouse paid Medicare taxes while working (premium-free Part A). Otherwise, there's a monthly premium.
- Deductibles and Coinsurance: You may pay deductibles and coinsurance for services.

**2. Medicare Part B (Medical Insurance)**

- Covers outpatient care, doctor visits, preventive services, and durable medical equipment.
- Cost: Requires a monthly premium (based on income) and an annual deductible.
- Coinsurance: Typically pays 80 percent of approved costs, with you covering the remaining 20 percent.

---

70 Little, Ryann. "Why Retirement Planning Should Include Medicare and Health Care Costs." National Council on Aging, July 2025. https://www.ncoa.org/article/why-retirement-planning, Accessed 9/24/2025.

3. **Medicare Part C (Medicare Advantage)**
    - A private insurance alternative to Original Medicare (Parts A and B), often including Part D coverage and additional benefits like vision, dental, and hearing.
    - Cost: Varies by plan; may include additional premiums, deductibles, and copays.
    - Networks: Plans may have specific provider networks (HMO or PPO).
4. **Medicare Part D (Prescription Drug Coverage)**
    - Covers prescription medications.
    - Cost: Monthly premium, deductible, and copayments or coinsurance.
    - Plans and costs vary; offered by private insurance companies approved by Medicare.
5. **Medigap (Medicare Supplement Insurance)**
    - Optional private insurance to cover "gaps" in Original Medicare, such as copayments, coinsurance, and deductibles.
    - Cost: Premiums vary by plan and location.
    - Cannot be combined with Medicare Advantage plans.

**Eligibility**

- Age-Based: Most people become eligible at age 65.
- Disability-Based: Eligible after receiving Social Security Disability Insurance (SSDI) for 24 months.
- Medical Condition-Based: Immediate eligibility for ESRD or ALS.

**Enrollment Periods**

- Initial Enrollment Period (IEP): Starts three months before your 65th birthday, includes the birthday month, and ends three months after.
- General Enrollment Period (GEP): January 1–March 31 annually, for those who missed their IEP.
- Special Enrollment Periods (SEP): For qualifying life events, such as losing employer coverage.

- Annual Open Enrollment Period: October 15–December 7, for making changes to Medicare Advantage or Part D plans.

**Costs**

- Premiums: Based on income for Parts B and D. This works like tax tables and is called IRMAA (Income-Related Monthly Adjustment Amount)
    - IRMAA is an additional charge added to the standard premiums for Medicare Part B (medical insurance) and Medicare Part D (prescription drug coverage) for higher-income individuals and couples. It's based on your Modified Adjusted Gross Income (MAGI) from two years prior, as reported on your tax return.
- Deductibles: You must meet a deductible before Medicare starts paying for services.
- Copayments/Coinsurance: Shared costs for services, typically a percentage.

**What Medicare Doesn't Cover**

- Long-term care.
- Routine dental, vision, or hearing care (covered by some Medicare Advantage plans).
- Overseas medical care.
- Cosmetic surgery.

IRMAA is extremely important when it comes to retirement planning for many individuals because it can become an additional expense that you continue to pay throughout your retirement if you are in the higher tax brackets. For that reason, it is worth diving in deeper by asking some questions:

**1. Who Pays IRMAA?**

- Individuals with higher incomes are subject to IRMAA. The thresholds are based on your filing status (e.g., single, married filing jointly) and your MAGI (modified adjusted gross income).
- MAGI includes your adjusted gross income (AGI) plus tax-exempt interest.

2. **How Is IRMAA Calculated?**
    - The Social Security Administration (SSA) determines IRMAA amounts annually, using tax return data from two years earlier. For example:
        - Your 2025 IRMAA is based on your 2023 MAGI.
    - If your income exceeds certain thresholds, you'll pay higher premiums for Medicare Part B and/or Part D.
3. **What are the Income Thresholds?** Income thresholds may be adjusted annually for inflation. Examples below are from 2026.
    - Single filers: MAGI above $109,000.
    - Married filing jointly: MAGI above $218,000.
    - Higher tiers: As income increases, so do IRMAA charges.
4. **How Much Is IRMAA?**
    - Medicare Part B: Standard premium increases by a set amount based on income tier. IRMAA for Part B can significantly raise your premium.
    - Medicare Part D: Adds a surcharge to your plan's standard premium.
    - Higher-income beneficiaries could pay hundreds of dollars more each month.

If your income has decreased due to specific life events (e.g., retirement, divorce, loss of income), you can appeal the IRMAA determination by filing Form SSA-44 ("Medicare Income-Related Monthly Adjustment Amount - Life-Changing Event"). Valid reasons include:

- Retirement or reduced work hours.
- Death of a spouse.
- Loss of income-producing property.

Although you can appeal IRMAA, it is not promised that your appeal will be accepted. Planning ahead can make a big impact on potential increases.

Here are some planning tips that can come in handy:

1. **Tax Planning:** Strategically manage income sources (e.g., Roth conversions, tax-efficient withdrawals) to stay below IRMAA thresholds.

2. **Withdrawals:** Use funds from Roth IRAs or other tax-free accounts that don't count toward MAGI.
3. **Timing Income:** Be cautious of large, one-time income events (e.g., selling property or realizing large capital gains) that could push you into a higher IRMAA bracket.

## Long-term Care

According to the Department of Health and Human Services, an estimated 56 percent of Americans turning 65 are likely to develop a condition requiring long-term care.[71] So, what exactly does that mean? Doesn't Medicare cover that? The short answer is no; Medicare does not cover long-term care (LTC).

Medicare defines long-term care as "custodial care" and most nursing home care is custodial care. This can be a range of services and support for your personal care needs. Typically, LTC isn't medical care, it is basic personal tasks used in everyday life like bathing, dressing, and using the bathroom. These are also called "activities of daily living" which for most long-term care policies, you'll qualify for if you can't perform two out of the six activities of daily living.

We had a family member that had been married for about 40 years. The husband was a bit older than the wife and had developed cancer. Everything was done that could be done to treat him and elongate his life. However, this was expensive and cost quite a bit. His wife ended up outliving him by 20 years and towards the end, she needed memory care from a facility to help her because of dementia. There was not much money left at that point when she ended up needing memory care, and memory care facilities are typically the most expensive place to be. Unfortunately, spending a large amount on the healthcare of an ailing spouse to then have the surviving spouse left with depleted funds happens all too often. It is important to plan before it happens.

---

71 Benz, Christine, "How Likely Are You to Need Long-Term Care?" Morningstar, July 2024, https://www.morningstar.com/retirement/how-likely-are-you-need-long-term-care, Accessed 9/24/2025.

***Fast Fact:*** *Three in five Americans—or 57%—say they regret a financial decision they made because of misinformation.*[72]

***Options to Pay for Long-Term Care***

There are three main ways to pay for long-term care, and many people mix and match to combine them as needed. The three different methods are Medicaid, Long-term Care Insurance, and Self-Pay.

Medicaid is a government program that will help pay for nursing homes, assisted living, or in-home care for people who meet specific income and asset limits. Each state varies on these limits, but there are general rules that apply. The income limit for 2025 was around $15,650 per year for an individual, or $32,150 per year for a family of four.[73] In addition to the income limit, most states also limit your countable assets (cash, savings, investments) to $2,000. They do not count your home (if it is under a certain value), one car, and your personal belongings (furniture/clothing) as part of that $2,000. These limits can increase if you are married, but the assets allowed are still capped.

There is also a five year lookback period to count the assets, meaning that Medicaid will look at your financial records over the past five years to make sure that you didn't try to give away or "hide" your assets from them to qualify for Medicaid. One strategy that some retirees use if they plan on using Medicaid is an irrevocable Medicaid trust. This moves your assets into a trust at least five years before Medicaid looks at your financials, with the purpose of taking your assets out of your name so that you qualify for Medicaid. Medicaid is intended for those who need long-term care but can't afford it.

Long-term care insurance (LTCI) is another option that is designed to help cover the costs of in-home care, adult day care,

---

72 CFP Board, Steering Clear of Financial Misinformation: A Survey of Americans, April 2025, https://www.cfp.net/knowledge/reports-and-statistics/consumer-surveys/steering-clear-of-financial-misinformation-survey, Accessed 6/27/2025

73 Federal Poverty Level (FPL)." Healthcare.gov. 2025. https://www.healthcare.gov/glossary/federal-poverty-level-fpl/, Accessed 9/24/2025.

assisted living, or nursing homes. It provides a financial safety net for you and your spouse to prevent you from relying solely on family assistance or personal savings, thereby preserving your wealth. Traditional LTCI policies have seen substantial declines in the industry while hybrid LTCI policies have been used more and more. There are many reasons for this, but let me explain a few.

Traditional LTCI policies are generally based on reimbursement now, where the owner pays for the costs out of pocket for the long-term care, then submits the receipts. The receipts are then reviewed against the contract, and the covered items are reimbursed up to the maximum benefit amount allowed (which is a hassle).

Traditional LTCI can also be expensive to buy, and the annual premiums can go up when the insurance company feels they need to raise rates to keep them cost-effective, very similar to car insurance. Many of the policies are also written in a way that if you don't use it, you lose it, so someone could pay into the policy their entire life and not get anything back, even at death.

Hybrid policies have become more popular because they are additions or "riders" onto other insurance policies like a life insurance policy or an annuity. Often with these, they are indemnity plans where there is a maximum monthly benefit given regardless of the actual cost of care. This way, if you need long-term care and qualify for it, you submit the paperwork from your healthcare provider saying that you need the care, and they just send the check to you to use how you see fit.

In these types of policies, you will end up using the money that you put in one way or another, either for long-term care, retirement income, or as death benefit paid to your beneficiaries. Most often, LTCI is not intended to cover the full amount of a potential long-term care event. Instead, it's used to help supplement the cost by giving the policy owner extra income so their savings are not drained as much or as quickly.

Here is an example of where and how a LTCI might come into play with the planning process. Carl and Cathy both work and live comfortably on $125,000 a year. They have retirement savings worth $800,000, are close to paying off their home, and have almost $40,000 in the bank. All of this is threatened when Carl suffers a critical accident that leaves him unable to fully care for himself. Cathy takes care of Carl in the evenings, nights, and weekends, but she can't stay home during the work day because her job is the only source of income they now have. Cathy arranges for Carl to receive a combination of adult day healthcare and home healthcare that frees her to keep working, but it costs over $4,000 a month.

Fortunately, Carl and Cathy have a life insurance policy with a long-term care rider that pays for home-based care and community-based care, in addition to facility-based care. It pays about $3,000 of Carl's monthly long-term care expenses, and Cathy is able to pay the rest out of her income so that they don't have to tap their retirement funds. Thanks to their long-term care insurance coverage, Carl and Cathy can handle this change in circumstances without threatening their long-term financial security. It's in this kind of situation that long-term care insurance does its best work.

Self-paying for long-term care is the third most common way to cover it. The median cost of a private room at a nursing home facility was $127,750 annually in 2024, and an assisted living facility was $70,800 annually in 2024.[74] For adults over 65 years old, 10 percent are expected to have long-term care needs that last less than a year, while 22 percent are expected to have needs that extend beyond five years.[75]

Paying for long-term care can be expensive, however, if you have the savings built and a modest lifestyle compared to your savings, you might be able to cover the financial strain of a long-term care incident and still meet your legacy planning goals. *The key is to plan ahead.* What planning ahead often looks like is running multiple simulations using financial calculators that can

74 Genworth Financial, Inc. "Genworth and CareScout Release Cost of Care Survey Results for 2024." Press release, March 2025. https://investor.genworth.com/news-events/press-releases/detail/982/genworth-and-carescout-release-cost-of-care-survey-results, Accessed 9/24/2025.

75 American Association for Long-Term Care Insurance, "Long-Term Care Need Data for Men and Women," July 2024, https://www.aaltci.org/long-term-care-need, Accessed 5/23/25.

depict what your portfolio will look like in good and bad markets, then add the income plan and add a long-term care incident into the projection.

Once you determine that you can afford to self-pay, the best practice is to set the money aside for the long-term care. Invest with purpose in this bucket and don't plan to touch it unless necessary. You will retain full control of the money, and it will be liquid without needing to "qualify" for long-term care.

Here is an example of where self-paying for long-term care might make the most sense. Steve and Sarah are about to retire after they have been living comfortably on $150,000 income per year. Sarah has saved $600,000 in her employer's retirement plan, Steve has saved $500,000 in his SIMPLE IRA, and Steve just sold his business for $1.5 million, giving them $2,600,000 in savings towards retirement. Their combined Social Security will be $60,000 and Sarah has a pension that will be $28,000 per year.

Their home is paid off and they have a second home by the beach worth $350,000 that they plan to use in retirement and should be paid off in about five years. If Steve or Sarah were to become sick and need long-term care, they would have enough assets compared to their lifestyle to be able to afford the cost of care out of pocket. At this point in their life, the purpose of LTCI would be to protect the inheritance that they will be leaving behind, which is why it would be more of a *want* than a *need*.

## Conclusion

As you weigh your options for healthcare in retirement, you need to consider not only yourself, but the people you love. Do you want to potentially burden a spouse or your loved ones with your long-term care costs that potentially put their own retirements at risk? Do you want to burden them physically and emotionally? Do you want to put yourself at the mercy of the Medicaid system? Or do you want to plan ahead by either getting long-term care insurance or a life insurance solution that can help you get the care you deserve?

By working with a financial professional, you can tailor a solution that makes the best use of your money and allows you and your family to be prepared for a long-term need should one arise.

## CHAPTER SEVEN CHALLENGE:

Before you make a decision about how to plan for long-term care, ask yourself the following questions below:

Have you considered early retirement? If so, what are your plans for healthcare coverage?

________________________________________________

________________________________________________

________________________________________________

Have you included Medicare costs in your retirement income plan?

________________________________________________

________________________________________________

________________________________________________

Will you choose a Medicare supplement or Medicare Advantage?

________________________________________________

________________________________________________

________________________________________________

Is long-term care a concern of yours? Why?

________________________________________________

________________________________________________

________________________________________________

If you will need long-term care in the future, how will you pay for it?

________________________________________________

________________________________________________

________________________________________________

How will a long-term care event impact your financial projections for retirement? Can you afford it?

___

___

___

If you would like to discuss the impact of healthcare expenses on your retirement, please contact us using one of the contact methods below:

- By phone: (636)388-7722
- By email: Tom@RetirementWealthDesign.com

# CHAPTER EIGHT

## LEAVE A LEGACY, NOT A HEADACHE

*"You cannot escape the responsibility of tomorrow by evading it today."*
*~ Abraham Lincoln*

Anne Heche, a renowned actress, died in August 2022 without a formal **will**, which led to legal disputes over her estate. Her oldest son, Homer Laffoon, filed to be the estate's administrator because he claimed that she did not have a will. However, her former partner, James Tupper, contested this, bringing up a 2011 email from Heche expressing her wish for Tupper to manage her estate. Tupper also questioned Laffoon's capability to serve as administrator due to his age and financial status. Additionally, Lynne Mishele, whose residence was destroyed in the crash that led to Heche's death, filed a $2 million lawsuit against the estate.

In November 2022, the court appointed Laffoon as the general administrator. By early 2024, the estate faced debts exceeding $6 million, including Mishele's claim.

This situation underscores the importance of having a clear and legally recognized estate plan. Without one, even informal communications, like Heche's 2011 email, can lead to prolonged legal battles and financial complications for surviving family members.

Estate planning might be the most important decision you will make in your life. Estate planning is not only about what happens when you die, but about what happens when you are alive. It is far too important to put off, and if you are still working, you might have legal benefits through your employer that will offer estate planning at a very discounted price.

There are many reasons to estate plan, but here are what I believe are the core reasons. It will provide you with control over your financial and medical decisions while you are alive and after passing. It will document your intentions and transfer assets to the appropriate people or trusts. Estate planning now will simplify the process later and provide you with peace of mind by removing conflicts. There are also potential tax advantages to estate planning!

---

***Fast Fact:*** *Only 24% of Americans have a will.*[76]

---

## Probate

**Probate** is what beneficiaries do not want to deal with after you pass. It can make mourning difficult and as your property gets trapped in probate, often beneficiaries need to pay out of pocket to cover costs of your estate until probate is resolved. Probate court can typically take six to 12 months to resolve if it's a straightforward case. If it's not a straightforward case or is a complex estate, then it can take significantly longer.

The purpose of probate is to administer a deceased person's estate by ensuring debts are paid and assets are distributed according to the deceased's will. If no will exists, then assets are distributed according to state law. One of the most common misconceptions is that if you have a valid will in place, then your assets will avoid probate. This is *not* true. A will directs the probate court on what your wishes are to distribute your assets.

When you have a will, your items will still go to probate, the court will validate the will and then form a trust to distribute the assets. The formation and administration of that trust, called a testamentary trust, can be expensive, typically costing approximately five percent of the value of the estate.

76 Lurie, Victoria. 2025 Wills and Estate Planning Study, Caring.com https://www.caring.com/caregivers/estate-planning/wills-survey/ Accessed 2/18/2025.

Probate is typically required when the deceased person's property is solely in their name (not jointly or in a trust), there are no beneficiaries listed, the value exceeds state limits, or there are disputes among creditors/heirs. In the state of Missouri, for example, the estate value must be greater than $40,000 to require probate. If the value of the estate is less than $40,000, it can qualify for a simplified probate process that is less cumbersome, much faster, and reduces the number of required court appearances.

## Avoiding Probate

To begin to understand how to avoid probate, first we need to know what happens to your assets upon passing. First, your accounts will be distributed according to the operation of law. Property that is held jointly (in the name of more than one person) will pass according to state law. If it is a "tenants in common" state, then the share of the property owned by the deceased will be distributed according to their wishes or probate. If it is a "tenants by entirety" state, such as Missouri, then the property is considered 100 percent owned by all named owners on the account, so the account will pass immediately to the other owner and avoid probate.

Next, if there is a "Transfer on Death" (TOD) for the property, then the property will avoid probate and go directly to the named person/organization. This is often done for vehicles through the DMV and bank accounts through the bank.

The second way that property can avoid probate is with a beneficiary designation. This is why it is so important to check your beneficiaries listed on your accounts regularly! I once met a gentleman that had been remarried for nine years, however, when we looked at his 401(k), it surprised both he and his new wife that he still had his ex-wife listed as the beneficiary! Suffice it to say, that the conversation got a little tense that day.

When a beneficiary is listed on the account, and that beneficiary is competent in the eyes of the law, then the property will avoid probate and go directly to the beneficiary. Employer retirement plans, IRAs, and ROTH IRAs are common types to list beneficiaries on. An asset that can be overlooked is your real estate. You can have a beneficiary deed on your home so that it will also avoid probate. Beneficiary deeds are often either written by an attorney or can be completed through your county's recorder of deeds office.

If you own real estate that is in a different state, please check with that state's laws and do pro-active planning, because when out-of-state real estate goes to probate, it typically means that the heir will have to fly there multiple times to attend court.

The third strategy to avoid probate court is by bequest. This is done through a will and/or trust. Again, if only a will is in place, the property will still go to probate. However, when a trust is written and the assets are put into the name of the trust, probate can be avoided because those listed assets are now under the care and ownership of the trust. Then, the property owned by the trust will be distributed according to what is written in the trust documents.

Because there are so many ways to avoid probate, sometimes, all a person needs is a will. What I mean is that if all of your major assets such as your 401(k), IRA, Life Insurance, house, cars, bank accounts, etc. have proper beneficiaries on them that are competent, then all of your major assets will avoid probate and the leftover personal items can zoom through an expedited probate process. In this scenario, then a will might be the ideal plan for you. Why you would still want a will in this scenario is the protections that the will provides while you are alive – specifically the medical and financial powers of attorney, advanced directive, and D.N.R.

**WHAT GOES IN THE PROBATE POT?**

Source: Magellan Financial.

## Estate Plans Should Include

Estate planning requires a comprehensive strategy to manage and distribute your assets, protect your loved ones, and address your financial and healthcare needs both during your lifetime and after your death. The concept that estate planning is only for the "rich" just isn't the case once we really peel back the layers of what is included. Even the formation of a trust can be beneficial for those that don't consider themselves "rich" depending on the situation and if a trust would save them money and stress.

These are common aspects of an estate plan that a qualified attorney in your state will walk through with you:

**1) Will:** A will is a legal document specifying how your assets should be distributed upon your death. It allows you to:

- Name beneficiaries for your property.
- Appoint an executor to manage your estate.
- Designate guardians for minor children.
- Outline any specific wishes, such as funeral arrangements.

*Key Tip:* A will must go through probate, so consider other tools to minimize probate where possible.

**2) Living Trust:** A living trust is an alternative or supplement to a will that allows your assets to bypass probate. It involves:

- Transferring assets into the trust during your lifetime.
- Managing or distributing assets according to your instructions, even if you're incapacitated or deceased.
- Appointing a trustee to manage the trust.

*Key Benefit:* Trusts provide privacy, faster asset distribution, and reduced court involvement.

**3) Powers of Attorney:** These documents designate trusted individuals to make decisions for you if you cannot do so yourself:

- Financial Power of Attorney: Authorizes someone to handle your financial matters, like paying bills, managing investments, or selling property.
- Healthcare Power of Attorney: Allows someone to make medical decisions on your behalf.

**4) Advance Healthcare Directive (Living Will):** This document outlines your preferences for medical treatment if you are unable to communicate, including:

- Decisions about life-sustaining measures (e.g., ventilators, feeding tubes).
- Preferences for pain management and organ donation.

*Key Benefit:* This documents your wishes so that your loved ones don't have to make the hard decisions.

**5) Beneficiary Designations:** Some assets allow you to name beneficiaries directly, avoiding probate:

- Retirement accounts (e.g., 401(k), IRA).
- Life insurance policies.
- Payable-on-death (POD) or transfer on death (TOD) accounts.

*Key Tip:* Regularly update beneficiary designations to reflect life changes (e.g., marriage, divorce, new children). The laws can change, so consult your attorney to ensure your trust can be the beneficiary of your IRA/401(k) prior to listing it as the beneficiary if that is your intention.

**6) Guardianship Designations:** If you have minor children, an estate plan should include:

- Naming a guardian in your will to care for your children if both parents pass away.
- Providing financial support through a trust or other mechanisms.

**7) Plan for Digital Assets:** Include instructions for handling online accounts, digital files, and cryptocurrencies. Consider:

- Listing accounts and passwords in a secure location.
- Designating someone to manage digital assets after your death.

**8) Tax Planning:** Minimize potential estate and gift taxes by:

- Taking advantage of the federal estate tax exemption.
- Using strategies like lifetime gifting, irrevocable trusts, or charitable donations.

**9) Business Succession Planning:** If you own a business, include plans for transferring ownership or management:

- Designate successors.
- Outline buy-sell agreements.
- Provide funding mechanisms (e.g., life insurance).

**10) Regular Updates:** Life changes may require revisiting your estate plan, such as:

- Marriage or divorce.
- Birth or adoption of a child.
- Death of a beneficiary or executor.
- Significant changes in financial status or laws. It is recommended to have a review every five years.

**Fast Fact:** *Dubbed the "Great Wealth Transfer," studies estimate that $84.4 trillion in assets will be passed down in the next two decades.*[77]

## Inheriting Retirement Accounts

The laws around inheriting retirement accounts have changed in recent years, notably with the passing of the SECURE Act and the SECURE Act 2.0. For a retirement account that is now inherited (the original account owner passed after 2019), these are the rules regarding the inheritance:

**1) Types of Retirement Accounts**

- Traditional IRA or 401(k): Contributions may have been pre-tax, and withdrawals are generally taxable.
- Roth IRA or Roth 401(k): Contributions were made with after-tax dollars, so withdrawals are typically tax-free.

**2) Types of Beneficiaries**

a. Spouse Beneficiary

As the spouse of the deceased account owner, you have the most flexibility:

- Roll the Account into Your Own IRA: You can treat the inherited account as your own, allowing you to follow your own Required Minimum Distribution (RMD) schedule (starting at age 73, depending on birth year).
- Inherit as a Beneficiary: Keep the account in the deceased's name and take RMDs based on your life expectancy (if the deceased was taking RMDs).
- Withdraw the Entire Account: Withdraw all funds at once or over time. Taxes will apply to Traditional IRA withdrawals.

b. Non-Spouse Beneficiary

- For non-spouse beneficiaries, the rules are more restrictive:

77 Milken Institute, We Aren't Talking Enough About One Aspect of the Great Wealth Transfer, July 2024, https://milkeninstitute.org/content-hub/power-ideas-essays/we-arent-talking-enough-about-one-aspect-great-wealth-transfer Accessed 9/12/2025.

- 10-Year Rule: If the account owner died on or after January 1, 2020, you generally must withdraw all funds within 10 years of the account owner's death. RMDs aren't required annually but the account must be fully emptied within 10 years (unless RMDs had already begun for the deceased individual).
- Exceptions to the 10-Year Rule: Certain "eligible designated beneficiaries" (e.g., minor children, disabled individuals, or beneficiaries not more than 10 years younger than the deceased) may take distributions over their life expectancy.

c. Minor Children of the Deceased

- RMDs can be taken based on the child's life expectancy until they reach the age of majority (typically 18 or 21, depending on the state). At that point, the 10-year rule applies.

d. Estates, Charities, or Trusts

- If a retirement account has no named beneficiary, or the estate, charity, or a trust is the beneficiary, the distribution options are more limited:
- Five-Year Rule: For accounts inherited from someone who passed away before taking RMDs, the funds must generally be distributed within five years.
- RMD Schedule: If the account owner had started RMDs, distributions continue based on the deceased's life expectancy.

**3) Tax Implications**

- Traditional IRA/401(k): Withdrawals are taxed as ordinary income.
- Roth IRA/401(k): Withdrawals are tax-free if the account has been open for at least five years. Otherwise, earnings may be taxable.

**4) Additional Considerations**

- Required Minimum Distributions (RMDs):
    - If the deceased account holder was required to take an RMD in the year of their death, the beneficiary must ensure that the RMD is taken by December 31 of that year.
    - Failing to take RMDs on time can result in a penalty (currently 25 percent of the amount not withdrawn, reduced to 10 percent if corrected quickly).
- Beneficiary Designation Forms: These forms override wills and trusts, so it's essential to keep them updated after life events like marriage, divorce, or the birth of children.
- Inherited 401(k) Plans: If inheriting a 401(k), you may need to roll it into an inherited IRA to take advantage of flexible distribution options.

As you can see there are numerous rules when it comes to inheriting accounts, however, if you are working with a financial planner, they will be able to walk through the process a step at a time to make it easy and do the heavy lifting for your beneficiaries. Typically, they will consult with the beneficiary throughout this process and give advice on the most tax efficient way to process and receive the funds.

Let's look at an example of how the inheritance of a pre-tax account, such as an IRA, will be received and taxed to the beneficiary. Jack Smith just lost his mother and is inheriting her Traditional IRA with an account value of $1,000,000. Jack is the only child and beneficiary listed, single, 35 years old, and works as an I.T. engineer making $150,000 salary per year. Jack chooses to take the money out of his inherited IRA over the 10-year period, taking $100,000 per year. The inheritance will be taxed as income in the year that Jack takes it.

Because it is added to his working income, some of Jack's inheritance will be taxed at the 24 percent level, but most of it will be taxed at the 32 percent federal level. On the million-dollar inheritance, Jack will pay approximately $272,460 in federal taxes.

If Jack were to live in a state that also has income tax, Jack would have to pay state income tax on the withdrawals as well.

So, what could Jack's mom have done differently so that Jack would receive more of the inheritance that she worked so hard to save and grow? She could have performed ROTH conversions while she was alive, especially if she was in a lower tax bracket, and had a lesser tax impact on the funds. If she was taking money out of a ROTH or taxable account while she was alive, she could have shifted her income plan while she was alive to take from the IRA instead of the ROTH/taxable accounts.

The third option would have been that she could have gotten a life insurance policy with a death benefit of $272,460 to pay the taxes on the million-dollar inheritance, because the life insurance death benefit would have been tax free.

## Common Types of Trusts

There are numerous types of trusts depending on the situation that you have and different ways that they can be structured. In this section, I am going to review what I believe are the five most common types. The important terms as it relates to trusts are:

- The grantor: The person that set up and put the assets into the trust.
- The trustee: The one who holds and manages the trust assets for the benefit of the beneficiaries.
- The beneficiaries: The ones who receive the assets in the trust.

The first type of trust is a revocable living trust. The purpose of this trust is to avoid probate and maintain control over assets during the grantor's lifetime. Because it is "revocable", the grantor can change or revoke the trust at any time. The trust becomes irrevocable upon the grantor's death, and the assets in the trust bypass probate, allowing for faster distribution to beneficiaries. It is typically best for people who want flexibility, privacy, and a streamlined estate settlement process.

For example, a person transfers their home and investments into a trust but retains control while alive. After death, the trustee distributes the assets directly to the named beneficiaries without court involvement.

The second type of trust is an irrevocable trust. The purpose of this trust is to provide tax benefits, asset protection, and ensure the grantor no longer controls the assets in the trust. It cannot be modified or revoked without the beneficiaries' consent because it removes the assets from the grantor's taxable estate. This, in turn, can protect assets from creditors or lawsuits. It is typically best for those with significant wealth seeking estate tax reduction or asset protection.

For example, a person creates an irrevocable trust for their children, transferring life insurance or high-value assets into it to reduce estate taxes.

The third most common type of trust is a testamentary trust. The purpose of this trust is to distribute the assets according to specific instructions after the grantor's death. These are created through a will and only come into effect when the grantor dies. The assets don't avoid probate because it's tied to the will, but can include detailed instructions like staggered distributions for minor children (they get half at 30 years old and half at 40 years old). These are typically best for people who want to provide a structured inheritance but aren't concerned about probate.

For example, a parent specifies that their estate will go into a trust for their minor children with distributions only allowed when they turn 25, 30, and 35 years old.

The fourth common type of trust is a special needs trust. These are generally used to provide financial support for a person with disabilities so that the financial support doesn't affect their eligibility to receive government benefits. They are managed by a trustee (someone other than the beneficiary/person with the disability) who ensures the beneficiary receives the supplemental funds for specific needs like education, travel, or medical care. The assets in the trust do not count as income or towards asset limits for the beneficiary so they can still qualify for government programs like Medicaid and Supplemental Security Income (SSI). These are best used for families with a loved one who has a disability or relies on government assistance.

For example, parents set up a trust to ensure their disabled child receives financial support without losing access to Medicaid, even long after the parents have passed.

The fifth most common trust is a charitable trust. The purpose of this is to support charitable causes while providing tax benefits to the grantor. The trust can provide income to beneficiaries for a period of time before donating the remaining assets to a charity, and the grantor can take the tax deduction for the charitable gift. The two common types are Charitable Remainder Trust (CRT) where it pays income to non-charitable beneficiaries first, leaving the remaining funds in the trust for the charity, and Charitable Lead Trust (CLT) where it provides income to the charity first, with the remainder going to other beneficiaries. It is best used for those that want to leave a philanthropic legacy while also reducing estate or income taxes.

For example, a person donates highly appreciated stock to a CRT, receives an income stream for life, and reduces capital gains taxes, with the remainder going to their favorite charity.

| | | MONTHLY | ANNUAL |
|---|---|---|---|
| **BASELINE** | Take Home Pay | $ 10,000 | $ 120,000 |
| | Savings from Take Home Pay | $ (1,000) | $ (12,000) |
| | | | |
| | | | |
| **DEBTS PAID OFF BY RETIREMENT** | | | |
| | Automobile | $ (1,000) | $ (12,000) |
| | Mortgage (Principal & Interest Only) | $ (2,000) | $ (24,000) |
| | | | |
| **ADDITIONAL RETIREMENT EXPENSES** | | | |
| | Travel | $ 833 | $ 10,000 |
| | Club Membership | $ 1,000 | $ 12,000 |
| | Medicare | $ 1,042 | $ 12,501 |
| | | | |
| **RETIREMENT INCOME TARGET (AFTER-TAX)** | | **$ 8,875** | **$ 106,501** |

Source: Author's own calculations.

It is also important to note that with these different types of trusts, there can also be multiple provisions based on your situation or need. For example, I come across families that may have a child with previous substance abuse, and the parents don't feel comfortable leaving substantial amounts of money to be received all at once. In other cases, a child may not be financially responsible, or they may be married to someone the parent doubts will be a long-term partner. There are multiple scenarios that can bring up reasons why specific provisions might be included, but let's discuss a few that might apply.

Provisions might include a lump sum payment to specific beneficiaries and spread out to others at defined ages. However, within these provisions, there may be an exception that the funds can be used on certain needs like health, education, maintenance, and support.

Other provisions can specify how you want the trust funds to be managed, such as stocks, real estate, or reinvestment of the trust earnings. You can include spendthrift clauses to protect the trust from being claimed by the beneficiary's creditors, or misused by the beneficiary (they can't transfer or assign to someone else). You can specify that the trustee can sell, lease, or exchange the property of the trust without court approval, or pay the trustee a nominal fee for the work involved with managing the trust. You can include items like your new spouse is able to take five percent a year for income, but upon their death, the remaining funds are distributed to specified beneficiaries and no one can alter those beneficiaries.

I have had some that want to ensure their pet is cared for if they die, so they have a "pet trust" that designates a trustee to care for the pet while using the trust funds to pay for that care. As you can see, many items come up in the formation of a trust, so they are specifically written for your intentions.

## Conclusion

An estate plan is about more than just getting the right stuff to the right people; it's about ensuring that your wishes are carried out in the manner you choose. This goes beyond just financial matters to include your healthcare, the care for the people that you love, and even your pets. A solid estate plan will include components that allow you to accomplish what is important to you.

## CHAPTER EIGHT CHALLENGE:

Have you verified the beneficiaries on all of your accounts within the past year?

________________________________________________________

________________________________________________________

________________________________________________________

Have you placed a Transfer on Death (TOD) on your vehicles and bank accounts?

________________________________________________________

________________________________________________________

________________________________________________________

Does your real estate have a beneficiary deed or trust assigned?

________________________________________________________

________________________________________________________

________________________________________________________

Have you consulted with a qualified professional on whether you need a will and/or trust?

________________________________________________________

________________________________________________________

________________________________________________________

If you have specific wishes for your money and property after you pass, have you considered a trust?

________________________________________________________

________________________________________________________

________________________________________________________

If you would like to discuss your estate strategy with a financial planner to discover how different options might benefit you and/or your heirs, please contact Retirement Wealth Design for a complimentary consultation:

- By phone: (636) 388-7722
- By email: Info@RetirementWealthDesign.com

# FINAL THOUGHTS

*"Whatever you're working on, take small bites. The task will not be overwhelming if you can reduce it to its smallest component."*
*– Richard Russo*

I loved completing our first 1000-piece puzzle with my kids. It was a learning experience that included numerous highs and lows. When we first opened the box, they looked inside and were excited to get started! But then, as they began to pull the pieces out of the box and lay them on the table, they felt overwhelmed and wanted to quit.

That was when I explained to them my strategy for putting together puzzles that I have used since I was a little kid. I would start with finding the corners, then work my way around the edges. Anything that stood out as a unique color or shape that I saw, I would address right away and start matching up the pieces. I organized the pieces into piles by their category (size, color, etc.) and just worked them one at a time.

The same can hold true for designing your retirement plan – you might be excited that you are getting close to retirement or just retired. Then, when you start to go through your investment accounts, how to invest, where to pull money from, how to take Social Security, how to pay for healthcare, etc. – it can get overwhelming *quickly.* Even with this book's goal of guiding you through your planning, I understand it may still feel overwhelming. But just like with puzzles, I use a process that breaks it down step-by-step to, as they say, eat the elephant *one bite at a time*.

The very first step is to figure out what you want your retirement to look like (just like the picture on the box top of a puzzle). It is going to look different for everyone, so getting really clear on the direction that you want to go is important. The next step is to define the purpose of your wealth and savings – what do you want your money to do for you or your family? Once those two steps are done, then it is smooth sailing and just lining up the plan, running projections, and simplifying it as much as possible so that you can focus on the important things in life. When we combine tried and true methods with strategic positioning for the current state of the world, your income, investment, tax, healthcare, and legacy plans are aligned for the peaks and valleys that are sure to come your way.

If I can be of service to you, whether it be answering questions, starting your plan, reviewing your plan, managing your plan, or filling in gaps in your plan, please call my office at (636) 388-7722 or reach out to me on my website, www.retirementwealthdesign.com. I will be happy to speak with you at no charge, to add clarity to your situation, and guide you in a **fiduciary** capacity.

You have worked your entire life, saved, and lived within your means. Retire comfortably, confidently, and in control so you can pursue your purpose and focus on the next stage. I hope that you enjoyed this book and are walking away better educated to make informed financial decisions. Enjoy your retirement!

# ABOUT THE AUTHOR

Tom Elder grew up in Saint Louis, Missouri where he now resides with his wife, Nikki, and two sons. At different points in his life, he has lived in California, Texas, and Florida, however, he and Nikki decided that when their twin boys were born, it was time to move back near family where they could grow up close to their grandparents and nine cousins. Tom spends his free time with his family, coaching sports teams, and being involved at church.

Growing up, Tom's values were strongly shaped by his parents and grandparents. He is the youngest of four, so in between attending his siblings' events, he played multiple sports including baseball, soccer, basketball, football and wrestling. He began working at the age of 13 years old and believes that his purpose through work is to positively influence the community around him. He finds joy and success in his ability to leave people better than before.

Tom attended college at the University of Missouri – Columbia, where he attained a master's degree. Since then, he has obtained his CERTIFIED FINANCIAL PLANNER® certification and educates his local community during multiple live educational workshops. He has been featured on local Fox and CBS affiliates, hosts local radio shows, authored multiple books, and has been called on as the financial planning expert witness for a jury trial.

Tom is the founder of Retirement Wealth Design, LLC, based in Saint Louis, serving clients around the nation. He created the company with intentionality, taking what he learned from his time working both at a national firm and a boutique firm, to create a business that was independent, upheld the fiduciary standard, and was focused on financial planning for retirement. He works with clients both before they retire and after they retire, building and executing fundamentally sound financial plans so the client can focus on the important aspects of life, knowing that they have an expert in their corner to lean on and guide them at all times.

# GLOSSARY OF TERMS

**ANNUITY** – An insurance contract where you exchange a lump-sum payment or series of payments in return for a regular income that begins either immediately or at some future date.

**BENEFICIARY** – An individual entitled to collect assets as decreed by a written, legal document.

**ESTATE PLANNING** – The simple process of moving money to someone else, including the transfer of assets, obligations, or responsibilities.

**FIDUCIARY** – A professional who holds a legal or ethical relationship of trust to prudently take care of money or other assets for another person.

**FULL RETIREMENT AGE (FRA)** – Also known as normal retirement age, this is the age at which you become entitled to receive your full or unreduced retired worker benefit from Social Security.

**HEALTHCARE DIRECTIVE (also known as a LIVING WILL)** – A document that spells out a specific directive of what you want to happen should a situation arise involving life-sustaining treatment. This document does not rely on the actions of another individual; rather, it gives the instructions directly to the doctor and medical staff.

**HEALTHCARE POWER OF ATTORNEY** – A written document in which you name someone (your "agent" or "attorney-in-fact") to make healthcare decisions for you if you are unable to speak for yourself. This person is then able to act on your behalf and carry out your directions for healthcare, without the delays of court proceedings.

**INFLATION** – The general rate at which the price of goods and services gradually rises.

**LIVING WILL** – See HEALTHCARE DIRECTIVE.

**PRINCIPAL** – The base amount of money that you put into an investment.

**PROBATE** – The legal process by which the assets of the deceased are properly distributed, the objective being to ensure that the deceased's debts, taxes, and other valid claims are paid out of their estate, and the assets are distributed to the intended beneficiaries.

**REQUIRED MINIMUM DISTRIBUTION (RMD)** – The minimum amount you must withdraw from qualified retirement accounts such as a traditional IRA by April 1 following the year you reach age 73 or 75, depending on the year you were born.

**RISK** – The danger or probability of loss.

**ROTH IRA** – Individual retirement arrangement made with income after the taxes have been paid where designated funds can grow tax-free with no taxes due on the interest earned if the contribution limits are followed.

**SOCIAL SECURITY ADMINISTRATION (SSA)** – A federal program in the U.S. that provides retirement benefits and disability income to qualified individuals and their spouses, children, and survivors.

**STANDARD DEVIATION** – A measure of a portfolio's volatility, also known as the wobble factor, and the most important thing affecting performance.

**TRADITIONAL IRA** – An individual retirement arrangement that provides a way to set aside money for retirement using contributions that are subtracted from your income (reducing the income taxes owed) and allowed to grow tax-free until the money is withdrawn, at which point taxes are owed on both the principal and interest earned.

**TRUST** – A legal document that creates an entity that is separate from you, designed to hold the title to assets while following a specific set of instructions for the management and distribution of those assets.

**WILL** – A list of instructions to inform a judge exactly how you would like your estate to be distributed, including your guardian preferences for underaged children.

Printed in Dunstable, United Kingdom

91228667R00107